Praise COURAGE BY DESIGN

"Values matter. Purpose matters. Vision matters. Not just for the people at the top of an organization. For everybody. The fact that Dee Robinson gets this is what makes *Courage By Design* such a masterpiece. Highly recommended."

—**Jerry Greenfield, cofounder,**
Ben & Jerry's

"Courage, perseverance, and determination is an individual choice that is made daily, and Dee's methods to success in all aspects of life are testimony that anything is possible when you put your mind to it."

—**Mindy Grossman, CEO,**
WW International

"Inspirational, aspirational, and a gift to all who choose bravery over complacency."

—**Suzy Whaley, PGA honorary president,**
PGA master professional, LPGA professional

"Dee Robinson's *Courage By Design* offers personal stories from admirable leaders on their journeys to courage. The book likens courage to a muscle that needs to get in condition and stay in condition through practice, and offers a practical, insightful method readers can use to build this strength in themselves. Dee's remarkable book can help you find your voice, pursue your dreams, and encourage those around you to do the same."

—Carolyn Dolezal, CEO,
The Committee of 200

"*Courage By Design* enables you to learn, from a great entrepreneur, how to lead with courage and integrity."

—Deirdre Quinn, cofounder and CEO,
Lafayette 148 New York

"We are heading into a time of great uncertainty. Our lives have been upended, our homes have become offices and schoolrooms, our political system seems hopelessly corrupted, social and global and climate unrest is outside our front doors and we don't seem to know anymore what the future might hold. But we do know this: what becomes of us individually is up to us individually; and what becomes of our society is up to us, too. Never have we needed more courage, and never has a book been more timely."

—Edie Weiner, CEO and president,
The Future Hunters

"Everyone who aspires to greatness should read this book. *Courage By Design* recounts the lessons that Dee Robinson learned in navigating and succeeding in a white-male-dominated business world. It will be pure gold in the hands of aspiring entrepreneurs and business leaders."

—David Weild IV, chairman & CEO,
Weild & Co., former vice chairman of Nasdaq

"A powerful and timeless message about the power of personal courage. Dee Robinson's transparency on how courage manifested in her life will resonate both with seasoned leaders and those just beginning their journey."

—Leslie Anderson, global head of employee tech experience, BMO Financial Group

"One thing we all need in life is the courage to confront our fears. In *Courage By Design*, Dee Robinson combines practical principles with compelling stories to show us how to lead purposeful lives that matter."

—Dr. Nicholas Pearce, professor, Northwestern University Kellogg School of Management and author of *The Purpose Path*

"This powerful book will position you to discover your inner courage and allow you to put that strength into action to create a better life for yourself and a better world for all of us. A must read!"

—Sam Silverstein, CSP, CPAE, author of *I Am Accountable* and *No Matter What*, past president of The National Speakers Association

"Nothing short of extraordinary. Dee shares how to face your fears, find courage, and be character in action in all things. Simply inspirational."

—Brad Vynalek, president, Quarles & Brady LLP

"Dee's book is insightful, impactful, and delivered with an unwavering heart. She *sees* how hard the struggle is, and she offers actionable game plans to help us show up stronger and more confident to keep going. Dee's voice is compelling and rings loud with truth, warmth, and humor. If you've ever been fearful at work, in your relationships, or anywhere in your life, you need to read *Courage By Design*. Dee will convince you to never give up on yourself."

—**Jane Hyo-Sung Park, CEO and cofounder,
Athena Consumer**

"Using powerful stories from visionary leaders, including her own personal journey, Dee shares a profound yet simple framework for living a life of joy, fulfillment and purpose. If you want to overcome fear, make bold choices and live your best life, *Courage By Design* is a must-read!"

—**Kirthiga Reddy, president,
Athena SPACs**

"Art imitates life, and I can see Dee parting the seas of excuses and distractions that are often standing in the way of your journey toward achieving success."

—**Nick Buzzell, CEO and chairman, NBTV**

"Among the key things I wish I had when I started out in business is a copy of this book. Dee Robinson's lived experience and deeply personal stories about the principles of courage make this book an imperative for anyone who wants to do better and be better, not just in business but in life."

—**Rodney Williams, former CEO & president,
Belvedere Vodka (LVMH)**

COURAGE

By Design

COURAGE

By Design

10+1
Commandments
for Moving Past Fear
to Joy, Fulfillment,
and Purpose

DEE M. ROBINSON

Published and distributed by:
SOUND WISDOM
P.O. Box 310
Shippensburg, PA 17257-0310
717-530-2122

info@soundwisdom.com

www.soundwisdom.com

ISBN 13 HC: 978-1-64095-402-1
ISBN 13 TP: 978-1-64095-404-5
ISBN 13 eBook: 978-1-64095-403-8

Library of Congress Control Number: 2022940029

For Worldwide Distribution, Printed in the U.S.A.

1 2 3 4 5 6 7 8 / 26 25 24 23 22

To My Mother

Helen Hill was many things: healer, friend, magician, caretaker, nurse aid, daughter, mother. She worked tirelessly, oftentimes two or three jobs at once. She had bills to pay, mouths to feed, and dreamed of more. I had everything I needed, not necessarily everything I wanted, but Helen made a way out of no way. The dream she may have hoped to pursue was not realized, I'm sure, for a host of reasons, for she lived in a time when a beautiful, smart, God-loving Black woman couldn't pursue her academic dreams, achieve financial success, or have the resources to do so. What she did was invest in her children. Her dreams were passed on to us, to me. Helen Hill is not a name known to you, but she was one of the most brilliant and wealthiest women I have ever known. She poured her heart and soul into me. This is her book; my business is her business. My life is because of her. I am proudly her daughter. Thank you, Mom. I miss you every day.

and to You

I know my mother would want me to dedicate this book to all those who struggle to find a courageous path in life, who know they have yet to find and walk that path consistently, and who ask themselves whether they really have the power to step out of a disempowering situation. If you have ever asked yourself that, even for a moment, I say to you: we all have the power to influence lives; we all have the power to influence our lives.

Whether it's changing your career or personal situation, facing a health challenge, leaving an abusive relationship, or overcoming the challenges of major economic obstacles, up to and including homelessness, I swear to you that you can make a way out of no way.

Courage is a choice, but not an easy one, and I dedicate this book to you and to your own personal willingness to make that choice. I dedicate this book to your own capacity to trust that you have the strength to take the first step toward fulfilling your dreams and building better circumstances in your life and the lives of everyone you touch. That step is simpler than you think: turn the page and keep reading. Take it right now.

Contents

Foreword

Dee Robinson is a leader who stands out in a crowded industry—hospitality. Why?

One reason is that she knows how to shake things up, how to move well-intentioned talk about (among other things) diversity, equity, and inclusion into strong relationships. I mean relationships that benefit both sides, create enduring impact, and deliver indisputable competitive advantage.

Another reason is that she's personally committed to leaving people and places better than she found them. This may sound like a common trait, but in my experience it's not as common as it should be, especially among leaders.

Yet another reason Dee stands out is that she knows what she stands for and she knows what her organization stands for. Put another way, she is not shy about talking about her values, enrolling others in those values, and building teams and entire organizations around those values.

What unites all of these reasons? Courage. As this book proves on every page, Dee has a PhD in courage.

Dee's is a powerful voice, a courageous voice, a voice to be heard. If you read her book and follow her guidance and example, she'll help you to shake things up, leave your world a better place than you found it, find and live your values, and make sure your voice gets heard, too.

Values matter. Purpose matters. Vision matters. Not just for the people at the top of an organization. For everybody. The fact that Dee Robinson gets this is what makes *Courage By Design* such a masterpiece.

My advice: Read Dee's book. Live her book. Stand out. And then do what she's done for years now: spread the word about exactly what it takes for each of us to master the art of courage.

—Jerry Greenfield,
cofounder of Ben & Jerry's

Prologue

I grew up making homemade roasted peanuts for my mother to sell in the stands of big league ballparks. Not long ago, a group of investors I was part of pursued a plan to purchase an interest in a big league team. I think about that and ask myself: *How does a journey like that happen?*

The answer came back in a single word: **Courage.**

When my siblings, Pearl, Michael, and Skip (Morris), and I were growing up, our mother always told us that the only kind of trouble we should ever get into was "good trouble." I believe this was because Pearl got into enough of the other kind of trouble. My mom was also talking about the kind of trouble civil rights icon John Lewis meant when he told people who wanted to make a difference in the world to "get in the way" and "get in good trouble, necessary trouble."[1] She always told us to leave people and places better than we found them and to find our own way, even though she knew that would not always be easy. That was her brand of courage. I took her words to heart.

The courage to follow my mother's example, to cause good trouble, took time for me to develop. It took practice. But that courage has taken me to some extraordinary and unexpected places—from airports to kitchens to the distillery to the executive boardroom and beyond.

As an entrepreneur, I have established a highly successful retail and food and beverage airport concessions management firm that has been busy for 25 years making life more enjoyable and food more delightful for travelers—and creating jobs and wealth along the way. Robinson

Hill owns and manages over 50 operations at some of the busiest travel hubs in the United States.

As a board director, I have brought my own business success to others and been able to champion issues of diversity, equity, and inclusion in a variety of industries.

As a public speaker, I have had the privilege of challenging a wide range of audiences to live their best life and actively work to become the change they want to see in the world.

As a facilitator of difficult conversations, I have provided safe spaces for people from diverse backgrounds to sit together and strive to hear and learn from one another in deeper ways. As part of that, I've written a cookbook, developed a conversation-starting game, and helped create a new bourbon, Good Trouble, knowing that sharing good food and drink creates an environment of warmth that can open people's hearts and minds in new ways. (A portion of the proceeds from the sale of every bottle of Good Trouble goes to select social justice organizations.)

All of that may sound like a collection of random projects, but some very important threads run through them all and weave together to form the tapestry of my life.

Everything I am involved in emanates from a desire to embody my mother's advice to change people, places, and the world at large for the better. And all of those activities have required me to be courageous.

From quitting a secure job in the corporate world so that I could go out on my own, to raising money to fuel growth, to being willing to pose the awkward, but important questions in business meetings, I have had to learn to face down my fears and step up if I want things to be different.

To make a difference, you have to be willing to step out of your comfort zone and take a risk. You have to be willing to risk running up against an obstacle, risk being hurt, risk being misunderstood, risk being rejected, risk being misrepresented. Courage is about change. Many people don't want change, don't think it is necessary, and can't handle it when it happens. You can't change the status quo without upsetting someone. But the rewards of a courageous life are worth it.

One big reason I wanted to write this book was to bring discussions about fear out into the open. Fear is like a dirty little secret. We all experience it, yet sometimes it seems like no one wants to acknowledge—let alone talk about—it. There is a strange taboo against acknowledging feelings of fear, against acknowledging the inescapable reality that courage does not happen automatically but is instead a matter of choice and careful planning. Being fearless doesn't mean an absence of fear; it means learning when and how to set fear aside so you can focus on something else you find more satisfying and fulfilling.

The **10 + 1 Courage By Design Commandments** reflect what I have learned and shared with others over the years about courage. Each commandment delivers an important principle for designing and living a courageous life, the kind of life that leads to fulfillment, purpose, and the true freedom that derives from becoming the person you are meant to be. By learning and practicing all 11 commandments, you too might just find yourself inspired to stir things up—to live the vision of your dreams.

Here is how to use this book: Start with Commandment I and work your way through the book. When you get to the end of a commandment, take some time to ponder the questions. Questions have the power to ignite deeper understanding. Once you have answered the questions, review and complete the simple action steps that follow. This will help you make meaningful connections with the ideas you've just read so that you can implement them successfully. Repeat the process for all the commandments that follow.

COURAGE
By Design

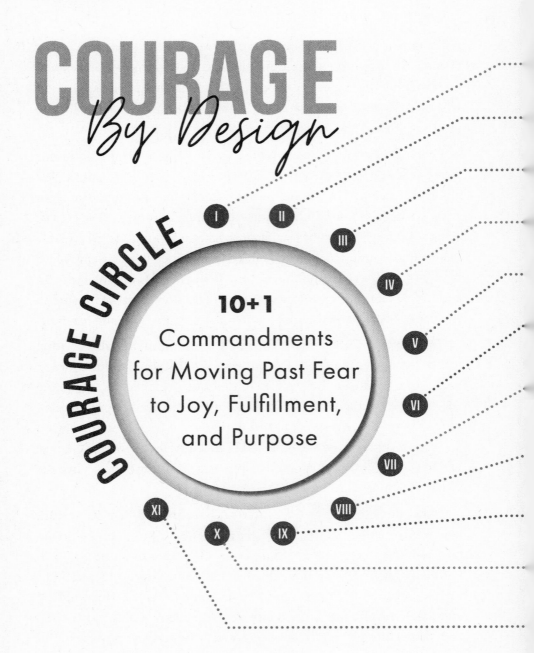

COURAGE CIRCLE

10+1
Commandments
for Moving Past Fear
to Joy, Fulfillment,
and Purpose

I   II   III   IV   V   VI   VII   VIII   IX   X   XI

	MIND MATTERS!	Assume Full Control of Your Thoughts
	TAKE CHARGE	Be the CEO of You
	ESCAPE	Break the Addiction to Fear; Practice Mindfulness
	BELIEVE	Harness the Power of Faith
	MISSION MATTERS!	Find Your Calling
	MAXIMIZE	Leverage Your Strong Suit
	CONNECT	Connect with Allies Who Are Focused on Solutions; Be Intentionally Curious
	BUILD THE CIRCLE	Choose Whom You Do (and Don't) Share Your Dreams With
	OVERCOME	Find Success in Failure
	SHARE	Your Secret Weapon: Give, Give, and Give Again
	INVEST	Make Diversity, Equity, and Inclusion a Personal and Competitive Advantage

We need courage more than ever in our world. My prayer is that by reading this book, you will claim your true courage. It's always there waiting for you. Courage is your choice and your right. I wrote this book so that it would not take you as long as it took me to learn to lean into your courage—and to thrive.

> "The cave you fear to enter contains the treasure you seek."
>
> —Joseph Campbell

COMMANDMENT I

Assume Full Control of Your Thoughts

MIND MATTERS!

"What consumes your mind
controls your life."

—Anonymous

1. STRENGTHENING THE COURAGE MUSCLE

"Our subconscious minds have no sense of humor, play no jokes, and cannot tell the difference between reality and imagined thought or image. What we continually think about eventually will manifest in our lives."

—Arthur Sidney Madwed

When I worked in corporate America after graduate school, I felt totally out of place. I was gripped with insecurity and fear. Was I doing a good job? Did company executives appreciate me, or like me, or even see me? I just didn't feel right in my own skin there. I worked long hours, I was tired, and I often felt overwhelmed. My malaise expressed itself physically as well—my body didn't feel right, and I was suffering from various health issues that I couldn't quite shake. Stress was taking its toll. All these signals were telling me something important. I knew deep inside that I needed to make a change, but for weeks—months—I kept stepping away from what I knew I needed to do: take control of my life by starting my own business.

I felt physically and emotionally unwell for one reason: because I had stayed for nearly a year in a job—in a world—that had provided me with wall-to-wall evidence that I was not in the right place. This world, for me, felt dangerous. So: Why had I stayed there as long as I had? Because of a lack of courage. I was afraid I couldn't pay my bills. It seemed like too big of a risk to leave.

Paralyzing fears, questions, and scenarios kept rolling through my mind: *What if I struck out on my own and failed? What if I invested in a business concept, then lost all the money? What if I went into debt?* Worst-case outcomes played over and over in my head.

Then one morning, while I was getting ready to go into work at a job I knew full well wasn't for me, I took a good long look at myself, and I had a moment of clarity.

As I stared into my bathroom mirror, I realized that I was asking questions that were not empowering me. That's one of the symptoms of a failure to take full control of your thoughts: asking questions that make you less effective, less likely to take action, less clear on how to bring your life purpose into reality as a contribution.

Again, I heard the disempowering question: *What if you fail?*

It was at this moment that I implemented a powerful formula for strengthening my courage muscle. In response to that disempowering question, I took a certain physical action—something very simple, something that I'll explain shortly. And once I did that, my whole thought process turned around. Things calmed down in my mind, and I started trusting that I would find the right path. I stepped away from worst-case scenarios and started asking myself different questions— better questions. The first question I asked was far more empowering. It is a question that has served me well on countless occasions in the years since:

What can I gain or learn from this situation?

I decided that I had not yet done my due diligence on this issue, and I resolved to find the answer to that question before I rejected the path of entrepreneurship.

When you ask yourself the right questions, the universe finds a way to get you the answers you need. That same day, I stumbled upon an article in *Forbes* magazine that changed my life. The article was about business leaders who had experienced massive losses and colossal business failures—but had rebounded.

I devoured it.

This article described the stories of several high-profile executives who had made horrific mistakes in their tenures at their companies' helms, including executives like former Quaker Oats Company CEO William Smithburg. Smithburg cost his company $1.4 billion dollars when he led Quaker into a disastrous acquisition of the Snapple drinks business.

Smithburg's experience, and the article as a whole, really put things into perspective for me: I might fail and lose any money I invested in my venture, but it certainly would be nowhere near the magnitude of a billion dollars. And Smithburg had gone on to achieve several successes post-Quaker Oats! Many of the people profiled in the article had experienced multiple bankruptcies but had proceeded to secure capital for major initiatives. They might have lost money, but they never lost their resilience, their talent, or their ability to dream big.

When I finished reading this article, I understood with crystal clarity that I was facing a pivotal moment in my life—and that up to that point, I had been asking myself all the wrong questions. Many, many others before me had taken risks that could have become monumental successes but instead became huge failures. Yes, I too might fail, just as they had. But if I did fail in my new undertaking, it would be at a far smaller scale. And if those people could rebound and come back stronger even after such devastating failures, I could certainly risk starting a business at only a fraction of that size—and I too could find a way to bounce back if I ran into problems. The skills those business leaders used to create their successes weren't lost. They used those skills to pivot.

I decided it was time to start my own company.

Let me be clear: I did run into problems. Big ones. I didn't get it right the first time. I wasn't *supposed* to get it right the first time. Each obstacle, each stumble, each failure was something I could use to strengthen the courage muscle—something that prepared me for the next challenge I would encounter and left me better equipped to manage it. The point is, as it turned out, the path of entrepreneurship, while not for everyone, definitely *was* for me. The decision to walk down that path never would have come about—and I never would have launched Robinson Hill, a successful airport concessions management company based in Chicago—if I had not put into action the formula I developed for summoning the boldness necessary to take full control of my own thoughts. I certainly would not be writing this book, either.

Are you wondering what I did to build up my courage muscle, to turn the disempowering question into an empowering one? Good. Keep reading.

2. THE SHAPE WE'RE IN

"Mental toughness is many things and rather difficult to explain... [It's] a perfectly disciplined will that refuses to give in. It's a state of mind. You could call it character in action."

— Vince Lombardi

Why is it that we so often know what to do but fail to take action? Why do we believe what we can't do more than what we can do? Let me answer those important questions by posing another:

What kind of shape are we in—not just physically, but mentally?

Courage is a muscle. In order to be able to use that muscle to its full capacity when we need it most, we must get into condition and stay in condition. This conditioning is mental.

Mental conditioning takes dedication and may even seem overwhelming at first...but that's only at first, before you've established what I call a *mental workout routine*. Once you pick up that routine and get used to it, getting into and staying in condition becomes a whole lot easier. That's just as true mentally as it is physically.

The first commandment of Courage By Design is here to get you over the hump. It's here to get you used to a regular mental workout routine that enables you to assume total control of your thoughts. You may think that assuming full control of your thoughts is impossible. I know I once did. But it isn't. My job now is to prove that to you.

There is a simple formula that I share with people I am coaching, one that is proven to work when it comes to getting into great mental shape—*if you practice it.* No one said it would be easy, but the outcome is definitely worth it. Once we *do* develop a mental workout routine that supports us, anything is possible.

Perhaps now you're asking: *What was the formula*? What did I do that morning right after I took a good, long look at myself in my bathroom mirror and heard my brain asking, *What if you fail?* What was the simple physical action I took that enabled me to turn my head around, start asking better questions, and eventually make a courageous decision?

It all started—my career as an entrepreneur, my charitable work, the book whose words you are reading right now—with a rubber band.

That morning, after I had taken a good, long look at myself, I snapped a small rubber band that I kept around my wrist. The tiny jolt of physical pain served as a small counterincentive for allowing a negative thought to occupy my awareness. That was the price I had promised myself I would pay every time I asked a question that did not empower me—every time I played out a scenario in my head that made possibility and opportunity seem small, and danger and difficulty seem large. I have conditioned myself to snap that rubber band whenever I find myself falling down a mental rabbit hole. I call this physically cued mental training process "SNAP-IT!," and it is an extremely effective means of reprogramming the mind to respond in a positive and constructive way to every problem or difficulty. In a moment, I will start coaching you to practice doing the same thing so you can build up your courage muscle, the muscle that minimizes fear and doubt when they start holding you back.

"Your strength will be in keeping calm and showing trust."

—Isaiah 30:15

Do I notice every single negative thought? No. Just like you, I am a work in progress. But I don't beat myself up about letting a limiting belief slip by.

Do I snap the rubber band the moment I *do* realize I've thrown myself down a hole? Yes.

So, that's what I did that morning. That's what empowered me to set aside fear and strengthen my courage muscle. That's what enabled me to keep my options open and ask a different set of questions—a better set of questions. This habit is deeply empowering. To this day, I wear a band around my wrist to help keep me focused, positive, and faithful. I also keep a supply of bands on hand and give one away when I encounter someone speaking limiting thoughts.

Today, let's start your own SNAP-IT! mental workout routine. I'm going to ask you to practice this every day for the next 21 days. By the end of the 21 days, the SNAP-IT! process will have become a habit and you will have made progress in conditioning your courage muscle to embolden you and support you in your success journey.

When a negative thought creeps into your mind, snap that rubber band and derail it. Give the thought a positive spin before it can take hold. Whenever you're faced with a challenge, use this formula. Let's say you're taking on a new responsibility at work, one that you've not had before. Use this formula to *instantly* replace "I can't do this; it's too much, too hard, too new" with "I *can* do this; it will contribute to my growth." Making mistakes is part of the learning process. Snap, reframe, and move forward!

You may get tired of snapping the band, but if you press forward and make this part of your daily routine, the reward will be a deeper consciousness of how your thoughts are influencing your life. Email me at dee@couragebydesign.com to let me know that you have made this commitment and to become a member of the Courage Community!

DO THIS

1. Get a rubber band and put it around your wrist.

2. Whenever you have a negative thought, simply snap the band on your wrist.

3. Then, as quickly as you can, find a way to rephrase the negative thought as a positive statement or question. (For instance, change the thought *What if I fail?* to the question *What can I gain or learn from this situation?*)

Go online to **www.couragebydesign.com** and download the free journaling tool I've created for you. It will support you as you make this part of your daily routine for the next 21 days.

A positive mindset is your right—your legacy. The three-step mental workout routine I have just outlined for you is the means by which you will claim that legacy.

Twenty-one straight days of thinking constructive thoughts will eventually shift your mindset, leading to more courage and motivation to help you advance your goals. Do not dismiss this technique because it sounds overly simple. Practice it for 21 days before you reject it. Open yourself up to what you are getting in these pages. Receive what is possible. This type of positive reframing can transform your life. It can create a new awareness in you that will invite new possibilities, new skill sets, and renewed hope.

Will it be easy for you to do this on day 1? Probably not.

Will you be a pro by the time you get to day 21? Absolutely!

DO THIS

Snap, reframe, and move forward!

Imagine you lived with someone who, day in and day out, every day of your life, 24/7, made a point of telling you how awful you are, how untalented you are, how improbable it is that you'll make a good meal, or successfully finish a paper that's due, or complete a convincing proposal at work. That would be horrific, right? Well, if you let negativity pervade your mind, that is essentially what your life is right now! You are listening to a voice that constantly belittles, criticizes, and demeans you.

If you put junk in, you'll get junk out. You'd likely divorce a partner who constantly belittled you and put you down; it's time to draw similar boundaries with your own inner critic. Tune that voice out. Commit to 21 days of SNAP-IT!

3. FIND THE BRAVE VOICE

"One isn't necessarily born with courage, but one is born with potential. Without courage, one cannot practice any other virtue consistently. We can't be kind, true, merciful, generous, or honest."

— *Maya Angelou*

Every person has two inner voices: a voice of fear and self-doubt and a brave voice. The voice of fear speaks failure and insecurity into your life, but the brave voice encourages you to face the unknown and inspire growth in yourself and others. If you listen well, you'll discover that these voices aren't separate streams of thought. The brave voice is simply the self-talk that results from acknowledging and reframing your limiting beliefs into fuel for your success.

I lived too many days of my life with fear and doubt attempting to paralyze me, but then I realized it was my job to tame my fears like a cowgirl taming a wild horse. The only reason I was able to start my company and live a life of contribution was that I learned to recognize the fearful voice I kept hearing as a guide to something better—an avenue for accessing my brave voice. That voice was (and is) a counselor, helping me to get clear on what I can choose to do next.

In order to get back on the horse, I need to develop what I call the *Courage to Hear*. I have to study the voice of doubt and insecurity, evaluate what it has to say, and then reframe its message so that it points me toward the brave voice. If I'm not listening to the brave voice, I reframe until I am.

> "Don't be afraid to start over again. This time, you're not starting from scratch. You're starting from experience."
>
> —Kareem "Biggs" Burke

Everything good in life starts with discovering your own brave voice, the voice that wants you to push your limits, to go a little further than you did last time, to think twice about whether you might be capable of something you thought you couldn't do. Whether you choose to listen to the brave voice is always up to you. The simple three-step SNAP-IT! process I have shared with you will make it far easier for you to change the frequency of your thoughts and tune in to that brave voice. Use SNAP-IT! to bring the voice of doubt and fear into the open, address it directly, reset, and take action on your aspirations.

At the end of each commandment, you will find *Courage By Design Questions and Actions*. These, along with the SNAP-IT process, will help you filter out the noise that is trying to keep you from strengthening your courage muscle and becoming the person you are meant to be. Remember, ignoring your inner critic is not the answer. By listening to the voice of fear and doubt and reframing what it is saying into a proclamation of your ability, you will be emboldened to take action on your vision of success.

"IF YOU'RE GOING TO DO SOMETHING, JUST DO IT"

I started out my career in sales with IBM in Dallas, Texas. I went through training with the group I had been assigned to. I got to know all the people in the branch. I worked there for about three years. And then my husband got an opportunity in Harrisburg, Pennsylvania. So we moved, and all of a sudden I found myself starting my career for IBM all over again in Pennsylvania.

I come into a new office, and I'm now more senior, because I have three years of experience…but I don't know anybody and nobody knows me. And the imposter syndrome started sinking in, because I told myself, *I have to prove myself—I don't know the ropes in this new office.* I'm not feeling confident that I know what I'm doing, despite the fact that I have three years under my belt. I'm listening to the wrong voice.

So I get a new account, and I see there is an opportunity that's been uncovered in that account. And I think to myself, *I have to make sure my proposal for this is absolutely perfect.*

Why? Because I don't want anybody in the Harrisburg office to think I can't do the job. I'm working extra hard, spending all kinds of extra effort doing every conceivable aspect of the research. I am coming up with multiple models for justifying the decision to go with IBM. I am leaving no stone unturned so people will see I know how to do this.

Lots of time goes into this proposal—not so much because I feel that's what is actually needed to win the business but because I want to prove that the feelings of inadequacy that are running through my mind about my new job just are not true. I dot every "i" and cross every "t." I find new i's to dot and new t's to cross that aren't even there.

What did it cost me? I ended up losing that deal. It took me far too long to put the proposal together, and by the time I presented it to the customer, he had lost the budget. If I had gotten to him earlier, we would have locked in the business.

I learned the hard way: If you're going to do something, just do it. Don't sit there and second-guess yourself. Don't make yourself do extra work because you're out to convince yourself—or even worse, out to convince others—that you belong where you are. When you find an opportunity, assume you deserve it. Take your shot! And remember: slow and perfect has a way of losing out to fast and workable, particularly in the world of sales.

—Shellye Archambeau,
speaker and author of the book *Unapologetically Ambitious*

Speaking of *just do it...*

4. BEFORE YOU MOVE ON TO THE SECOND COMMANDMENT, DO THIS

IMPORTANT: Your commitment to follow each Courage By Design Commandment is not complete until you have a) asked yourself the questions that show up at the end of the commandment, b) answered them *in writing*, and c) taken the actions that follow. You may choose to work with an accountability partner, which is a powerful technique that has delivered good results for me. That's up to you. You don't have to show your written answers to anyone or tell anyone what you've done unless you want to…but you *do* have to write down the answers and take the actions if you are serious about implementing this program.

QUESTIONS: COMMANDMENT I

- Think about your internal dialogue. What does it say to you? If someone else said to you what you said to yourself, would you push back (assuming it's negative)? Why do you think it's okay for you to say things to and about yourself that would be unacceptable if said by someone else?

- When you examine your day closely, are there any times you claim for yourself, time to be alone and quiet with your own thoughts? If not, is there a routine you could establish of taking some moments to yourself?

- What have you said *No* to today, or this week, that you could have said *Yes* to? Why did you say *No*? Did you toss away an opportunity to learn, or exercise, or recreate, or branch out? If so, what was it? Is a story from your past holding you back or defining you? If so, what is it?

ACTIONS: COMMANDMENT I

- Snap, reframe, and move forward! Commit to strengthening this mental muscle for 21 straight days, starting now. Bravely raise your consciousness about the quality of your thinking. Guard your thinking as an asset. It's a precious possession.

- Repeat as necessary: *I should be, deserve to be, and must be everywhere my dreams take me.*

- Find 10–20 minutes of quiet time each day. This is a must. You have the time. Use it. This is the secret weapon that will speed you along your courageous path. For help on this, visit www.couragebydesign.com and download the free Stillness Guide.

- Take a close look at your worry cycle. Identify three topics you worry about that are not under your control. Focus on what matters. Make a conscious decision to focus instead on matters that you can actually change.

Once you have done all this, you will be ready to move on to Commandment II.

COMMANDMENT II

Be the CEO of You

TAKE CHARGE

"Autonomy is different from independence. It means acting with choice."

— Daniel H. Pink

5.   BORN TO SLAY DRAGONS

> "We need to not be in denial about what we've done, what we've come through. It will help us if we all do that."
>
> — *Maya Angelou*

I chose to step away from a corporate career path that most people in my world considered "safe"…but to me, it was not just unfulfilling; it was dangerous.

Dangerous is, I know, a big word. Perhaps you're wondering: *Why did I feel that path I was on was so dangerous?*

Here's the answer: Because the path I was walking back then left someone else—someone I hardly knew and had no reason to believe I could trust—in charge of a huge chunk of my life. That path deprived me of *autonomy*, of *agency*…and it was not one I was willing to travel any longer.

Autonomy means the ability to make sound, informed choices based on what you know and believe without being coerced by other people.

Agency means the capacity to act independently and set your own course.

My decision to leave corporate America and begin a career as an entrepreneur came down to me drawing a line: I simply could not let someone who didn't care about me take control of my future. I decided to take the reins. I decided that I was in charge of my own life, no matter what happened. It was too costly to stay somewhere I was not valued.

DO THIS

If you're not valued, find a new place to be. Do not stay where you are not valued.

And that's what Commandment II—be the CEO of You—is all about. It's not (necessarily) about starting your own life as an entrepreneur. I would say "bravo" to any path that allows you to soar with your strengths and brings you joy. Others may tell you that staying with what is familiar is the best course…but your job now is to internalize and act on the reality that the real risk—the unacceptable risk—lies in handing the reins of your life over to someone other than *you*. This is *your* life, and the direction in which it proceeds is *your* responsibility, no one else's.

Launching and running a business is not for everyone. However we do it, we must all be prepared to reclaim the *agency and autonomy* that are our birthright as human beings.

We are each born with agency and autonomy. And we are each tasked with the responsibility of reclaiming them when we lose sight of them.

Reclaiming agency and autonomy means learning to work from the assumption that *you and you alone can be fully present and fully conscious in your own life, and you need no one's permission to do that.* You are the only person who can decide what is and isn't within your control and what your own experiences mean. Only you can learn to listen to the inner voice that tells you what should happen next in your life. That is why I asked you, in the previous commandment, to start taking quiet time for yourself each day. Quiet time is when we learn to recognize and heed that voice. Once you build up the Courage to Hear, you can build up the Courage to Dream Big, the Courage to Act, and the Courage to Do the Right Thing.

Embracing agency and autonomy means not blaming other people, not hiding behind other people, and not making excuses. It means taking on the role of Chief Executive Officer of your own life.

Regardless of what others may think or say about you; regardless of how, where, and when you choose to contribute; regardless of whatever is happening in your world right now, *you are the prime mover in your own life.* This is the reality of your existence: you are in charge.

Denying your autonomy and agency is like denying gravity. You can tell yourself whatever you want. But the fact remains: you are in charge here. And the sooner you set aside any narratives to the contrary, the better off you and everyone your life touches will be.

So, take the reins! Assume responsibility for identifying and making the choices that guide your life. *You* got yourself to this point. *You* will get yourself to wherever you end up next.

Today, you accept a promotion. Your title is now the "CEO of You"—and guess what? All of your adult life, you've actually held this high-level position! If you've ever bought into the belief that someone or something else held that job, that others control your destiny or hold the power to grant or deny you your future, let me invite you, with love, to hit "pause" now and take some time to critically reexamine your belief system. Some of your beliefs are not driving you toward greater success. In fact, some of your beliefs are holding you hostage.

Once you know you're at the helm of the ship, you accept the responsibility of running your own life. That means making brave, wise, sound decisions that improve your daily life and your future.

We are each the chief executive officer of all aspects of our lives: we are the CEO of our health, life, relationships, thoughts, and daily actions. Like all leaders, we must make hard decisions, and we must set the course of action. We must lead, not follow.

In this commandment, you learn to stop blaming, stop hiding, and stop making excuses. This is a major paradigm shift for most people, and it is often one that takes a great deal of courage. Stepping beyond what is familiar always takes courage. You have, right now, the opportunity to contribute, to make a massive positive impact, to totally transform the lives of others. Those opportunities are far more important than whatever story you may have been telling yourself about how you got here, what kind of luck you have had, or what person or external event is holding you back from doing what you could be doing with your life. Effective CEOs do not have time for stories that sap them of autonomy and agency. They learn to disengage from such narratives quickly. They put things in perspective.

> Effective CEOs do not have time for stories that sap them of autonomy and agency. They disengage from such narratives. They put things in perspective.

Just remember: Courage is not the same as not *feeling* fear…it is simply a conscious decision to set disempowering narratives aside and recognize something you want to do with your life as more *important* than fear.

Everyone has a list of what is not working in their life, a list of things that have gone wrong. The key is not to waste your time and potential replaying that list in your mind! Instead of thinking about what hasn't worked out for you, make a habit of thinking about the situations you have taken on and overcome. In the process, you'll become *curious* about whatever obstacle you find yourself facing. And this curiosity will open you up to hearing the brave voice that will carry you through to the other side.

DO THIS

Learn to be curious about your obstacles.

We are defined by our victories, not our defeats. Losing sight of that fact is the ultimate failure. When we encounter an adversity—any adversity—we have a duty to remind ourselves of all that we have bounced back from, all that we have overcome, all the darkness we have navigated our way through so that we can get some perspective on the challenge we are facing right now. This can literally be a life-saving choice, and we must make it—because not making that choice means robbing ourselves and others of who we are meant to be. It means blinding ourselves to strengths we haven't yet discovered or leveraged for a greater good.

We are survivors, you and I. We were born to slay dragons. If we close doors before they open because we think we are not worthy to go through them, that means we have forgotten who we really are. We have a duty to remind ourselves of our true identity as often as necessary.

If you have started a business, you started with net sales of *zero*. You changed that. Don't forget all that you did to build your business when it hits a bump in the road.

If you currently work as a member of a team, you started out with *no job*. You changed that. How? Through your choices and your actions. Don't forget all that you achieved if the promotion you were hoping to obtain doesn't work out. That's a temporary setback. *You are still in charge.*

You survived. You are still standing. You can choose to look at what's wrong and stay there, or you can choose to focus on solutions. When you are the CEO of You, you focus on solutions because you know *it is impossible to think creatively and solve problems when you are in a state of fear.* Use your thoughts to empower you, to make progress, not to keep yourself stuck.

Recognize that the next setback that comes your way does not define you. What you have accomplished, what you have solved, what you have contributed, what you aim to contribute next is what defines you. Do whatever it takes to remind yourself of that. Do it every single time you hit a challenge. There is no time to waste. There are dragons to slay!

6. EXECUTE!

"The future depends on what you do today."

— *Mahatma Gandhi*

The following personal testimony is one of the most powerful examples I have ever heard of someone choosing to assume personal leadership of their own life. My dear friend Lisa Stone is an accomplished investor, entrepreneur, speaker, and yes, CEO. Her awards and honors include Fortune's MPW Entrepreneur Award, Fast Company's Most Creative People in Business Award, and a Nieman Fellowship from Harvard University. Lisa has truly amazing parents—John and Janet Stone—and I am proud to be able to say I know them both. Listen carefully to what Lisa has to say about her journey of reclaiming autonomy and agency.

"YOU ARE SO, SO LUCKY"

When I was eight years old, my favorite uncle was discharged from the Army and came to live with us. One day, he invited me on a bike ride, just the two of us, to a huge construction site in our neighborhood. I got on my bike, he got on his, and we headed down a hill together. What he didn't know was that I'd just gotten my training wheels off.

We tore down that hill, and when I fell at the bottom, thank God my mouth was open, because my jaw literally saved my face. The accident, however, rubbed out my front teeth and embedded gravel and asphalt in my face and about 60 percent of my head, collarbone, arm, and right side. I went from being a nondescript little white girl into someone with metal things in her jaw who was very hard to look at and whom no one wanted to touch—unless it was for peroxide scrub baths. I lost track of how many oral surgeries, including bone and gum grafts, I had. (To date, I know that it's been more than 20.)

My second-grade playground became a nightmare and a gauntlet. I withdrew. I simply couldn't bear for anyone to look at me.

When my family of six went out to a restaurant—a rare treat, since my folks had had four kids in six and a half years and my mother put my father through med school on a teacher's salary—I sat *under* the table so that the other diners would not stare at me.

My deep-rooted terror of being looked at continued well after my face and skin healed. Then, one day, my mother Janet, a teacher and education specialist and genius people-whisperer, sat me down for a talk.

She looked me in the eye and said, "Lisa. You are so,

so lucky and fortunate. Your family loves you. You have enough to eat, and you are surrounded by opportunity. But every day we pass by people who are lacking. They are alone, and they are lonely. I think it's important that you reach out to them and say, 'Hello! Good morning!' Your smile and your caring about them can really make a difference. What if you are the first smile they see that day? The first kind word?"

Somehow she knew that the one thing that would get me to reach beyond my loneliness and isolation was the chance to touch another person who might be alone. As I say, she was an expert people-whisperer.

It worked. I moved beyond the nightmare. I got out of myself and began trying to watch for and reach out for a genuine connection with people who looked like they might feel or be experiencing isolation like I had. I think the idea of taking action on those opportunities to connect was why I became a reporter and a storyteller, two important stops on my life journey. I also believe my mother rocked me out of my privilege in a profound way the day she sat me down to talk to me, and that is something for which I remain deeply grateful.

—Lisa Stone,
entrepreneur and investor

In the moment Lisa decided to (in her words) "get out of herself" and find a way to contribute, she reclaimed the autonomy and agency that are her birthright as a human being. *You can do the same.* The space where Lisa, with her mentor's support and encouragement, chose to live is the space where *all* the remarkable people who have assumed true leadership in their own lives choose to live. You can choose to live there too, anytime you wish. But the price of admission is:

No more justifications. (As in, "I'm too scared of what people will think of me to put myself out there.")

No more "buts." (As in, "I would love to put myself out there, *but* I have so much going on today...I'll do it tomorrow." You don't know if you've even got a tomorrow to look forward to! None of us do! No loitering! Do it now!)

No more stories. (As in, "X, Y, and Z happened to me when I was a kid, so I can't do this.") Some stories disempower you and cheat the rest of the world out of what you have to contribute. What happened to you when you were a kid is just as over as the Napoleonic Wars. Find someone to talk to about the wars that have affected you, if that's what you need to do...but make sure the person you talk to is someone who will help you *move on.* Don't stay in grief or sanction sadness. Notice when a story makes you feel disempowered and *stop telling yourself that story. Don't become the story.*

> Don't become the story.

If you are going to be an effective chief executive officer of your own life, then you must meet the same five challenges Lisa met:

- *Listen carefully to a mentor or sponsor who is committed to your development and growth.* I'll play that role right now until you can find someone you can meet with voice to voice or face to face.

- *Cultivate gratitude.* If you can't find something to be grateful for in your world, you're not looking hard enough.

- *Get out of yourself.* Stop replaying failures, setbacks, and disappointments.

- *Find a place where you can contribute.* When you feel sad or defeated, get out and help someone else. You will start to feel the endorphins kicking in. Remember: Your mental state is a choice. Why would you choose misery? Why would you choose fear? When you find someone you can help and then get busy helping them, you are choosing connection, joy, and fulfillment. Keep making that choice, and you will build up momentum! Empowerment starts when you reach out and make a positive impact on someone else's life.

- *Start taking action—now!* This, after all, is what executives do. The very word *executive* directs you toward this point: executives execute! If you need some assistance, ask for help. No CEO does anything alone.

7. THE PLAYBOOK

"It always seems impossible until it is done."
— Nelson Mandela

For me, the year 2020 started out in grand fashion. The company I founded was celebrating its 25th year; over that time, I had grown it from zero employees to over 1,000, with annual revenues hitting the multimillion-dollar mark. I was poised for more growth in the year to come. Travel was booming; many of the airport restaurants in my portfolio were popular, sought-after, and highly successful; and it seemed like there were nothing but blue skies ahead.

Then COVID-19 emerged in February and began to spread, and we had to change course.

At first, we thought we'd be closed for only a couple of weeks; as it became clear that businesses would remain closed for extended periods of time, the pandemic became a major threat to my firm. Robinson Hill is an airport and travel venue concessionaire company, and when COVID-19 forced the cancellation of countless business flights and put the kibosh on travel and tourism, most of my airport businesses were shuttered long-term and many of my employees were furloughed.

With dozens of Robinson Hill-owned airport restaurants and retailers shutting down, we had to locate and divert massive amounts of inventory, much of it perishable. Revenues came to a complete halt, even as fixed expenses remained constant, causing a money-hemorrhaging situation. The cash flow was a concern, but it wasn't my biggest one. I care deeply about my employees and their welfare, and I knew they were hurting.

And then things got even worse. The horrific murder of George Floyd in May 2020 caused long-simmering social unrest to boil over; riots and looting broke out in multiple cities, and my heart broke again for all of those who experienced racism and injustice in almost every area of their lives. Just when we thought our collective situation couldn't possibly get worse, political divisiveness and the outrageous tactics and rhetoric of irresponsible leaders brought us into an ugly and sometimes violent season.

It's easy to feel small and defeated when you witness your company slowly crumbling, your employees seeking new jobs or filing for unemployment, and your country suffering a nervous breakdown. It's easy to feel demoralized at racial injustice and political hate speech. But soon enough I realized that feeling defeated or demoralized wasn't serving me or anyone around me. It was time to rise to the occasion.

It was time to set up and execute a plan for bouncing back, and that's exactly what I did—with the help of an ancient playbook.

I did what I could to help out as much as possible in the short term. I made sure we assisted employees in their efforts to file for unemployment, directed them to multiple resources like employers who were hiring and convenient food banks, and held several fundraisers to benefit them directly. I wrote articles, talked on panels, and spoke out in board meetings about the decimating effects of racism and how we must do better in corporate America by holding leaders accountable for a lack of diversity. All of this was productive, and it was assisting people in a meaningful way. Yet as much as I was doing, I knew I had to do even more. Where else could I use my skills and put my energy into what's next?

I had to go big. I had to find a way to help more people, particularly those who have been denied equal opportunity in the past, and I'm happy to say that I'm well on my way to doing that. Not only have I gotten Robinson Hill back on its feet in the post-lockdown period and begun rehiring some of the people we let go when air travel froze up, but I've also launched a number of new and exciting ventures that are bringing prosperity to underserved communities—notably the Good Trouble brand of bourbon. (You can learn more about that at goodtroublebourbon.com.)

In addition, Robinson Hill made fighting hunger a major organizational priority. Now, hunger is a complex problem. It can mean lacking food for a day or two on an occasional basis when paychecks don't stretch, or it can mean habitual food insecurity, leading to malnourishment, impaired development, and chronic disease. Hungry kids cannot learn; hungry adults cannot prosper. One in eight families is hungry, making up a staggering 12.3 percent of all US households.[2] Many people must choose between purchasing food and covering rent, mortgages, transportation, utility bills, and medical fees. And this problem, I realized, only got worse with the onset of the pandemic.

The point is, hunger is closer than many people think. That's why we developed Project Clean Pantry to help stock shelves at local food banks. Project Clean Pantry is a grassroots effort that encourages people to kick off their own local campaign to combat food insecurity in their area. By reaching out to neighbors, family members, and friends—which can be done on a virtual basis during times of social distancing—these individuals establish community groups that clean out their pantries and collect nonperishable items for group donations. These items are then brought to community food pantries to help stock shelves. We're now spreading the word on Project Clean Pantry through email campaigns and social media and via the hashtag #ProjectCleanPantry.

Long story short, the turning point in Robinson Hill's response to the pandemic came when I chose to *say to myself what I aimed to be.*

(This, by the way, is the best response to any obstacle; it's what turns an obstacle into an advantage.) The answer that came back was: *a bringer of opportunity and prosperity*...someone who shortens the runway to success for other people...someone who helps those in need. When faced with problems, I try to determine how I can be a help to others. This is the best possible therapy! When I do this, I am quickly reminded that my own problems are not so bad.

Shifting the focus to how I could help others, how I could leave people and places better than I found them, was both empowering and fulfilling! Helping people was obviously my role—not making myself and my company a victim of circumstance or the choices of others. Once I was clear on that much, my path was clear: reclaim my agency...do what I had to do in order to *reclaim my true identity* as someone who makes a contribution.

The pandemic took down a lot of businesses in 2020. Mine was not one of them. Why? Because I reclaimed the agency that was and is my birthright.

When I share these powerful ideas with people I coach—when I emphasize the importance of moving beyond justifications and limiting stories so they can reclaim agency and become the can-do, action-oriented senior executive in their own life that they were born to be—I tend to hear two predictable pieces of pushback, at least in the early going. The first is that what I am describing is somehow applicable only to entrepreneurs. And the second is that my insistence on making a *contribution* sounds like it applies only to the nonprofit world.

Read this next sentence carefully: **Both of these responses to what I am saying are *"buts"*—excuses for not moving beyond your present comfort zone**.

My challenge for you is to recognize them as excuses—as symptoms of a fear mindset—and then to set them aside. Seizing the reins of your own life is far, far more important than holding on to the "buts" that limit you as a person.

Take action! Claim your agency! Execute! If not now, then when? Don't wait for someone to validate you. Don't wait for someone to tell you it's okay. Do what you need to do, now! Don't wait until the conditions are just right. That time never arrives. All there is is NOW.

DO THIS

Claim your agency! Take action! If not now, then when? Don't wait for someone to validate you. Don't wait for someone to tell you it's okay. Do what you need to do, now!

Here, by the way, is a true story that debunks both of those "buts" I just mentioned.

A good friend of mine—I'll call her Carol to preserve her privacy—is a senior executive at a Fortune 100 company. Carol shared the following account of reclaiming autonomy and agency in her professional life.

"DON'T ACCEPT ANYTHING LESS"

When I first started working for this company, I was curious about how much I was making in comparison with other people who had the same level of responsibility

---

I did. But it was hard to come by salary data—senior management keeps those figures confidential—so for a while I was more or less flying blind. But I'm proud of the work I do, and I feel I should be compensated fairly for it. So I asked around.

For the longest time, I couldn't get any relevant salary data to compare my own package to. Then came the day when I happened to be out at a sporting event with a couple of friends, one of whom was a male colleague of mine working at exactly my level. At one point, he leaned over and said to me, "Look, I know you're interested in what I'm making, and I understand why you're interested. You've got a right to know what that number is." He told me what he was making each year. It was $100,000 more than what I was making! Then he said, "Don't accept anything less."

I didn't! I was a little nervous, but I went to my superior, told him what I had been contributing, told him how much I wanted, and stopped talking. It worked. And why shouldn't it have? Here was someone doing precisely the same job I was doing, delivering the same positive outcomes for the company, and he was earning that much more than I was. Why? Is it possibly because I'm a woman of color? Whatever the reason was, it was time for me to have a $100,000 discussion with my superior. And I'm glad I did.

—Carol

> ## DO THIS
> Summon the courage to get what you deserve. State your contribution and state your value; don't get distracted by anything else. Then…be silent.

Here's what I want to ask you now:

- Did Carol reclaim agency and autonomy in her professional life by talking to her superior? *Of course she did.*

- Did she have to quit her job and start her own company in order to do that? *No.*

- Was she focused like a laser beam on making a contribution at the highest possible level of which she was capable? *Absolutely! Wanting to be compensated fairly for that contribution is certainly nothing to be ashamed of—and she's not ashamed of it. I hope you're not, either.*

- Did she feel fear and apprehension? *Of course she did, but she took action anyway because it was the right thing to do. In that moment, she became the CEO of her own life.*

My challenge to you is to take the next obstacle, challenge, or difficult emotional exchange with another person that you encounter… and find a way to turn it into *fuel* for constructive action that moves you forward, that serves someone. How, exactly, do you do that? By giving yourself some perspective. By reminding yourself, over and over again, of what you've already overcome—and then becoming curious about the obstacle you face now. This is a critical skill when it comes to reclaiming agency. Failing to master that skill can have devastating consequences.

When I talk to people I'm coaching about reclaiming agency and autonomy in their lives—not just their professional lives, but all aspects of their life—I'm talking, fundamentally, about reclaiming *leadership*. No matter what you are doing professionally, you have a right and a duty to assume total, unchallengeable leadership in your own life.

The Greek philosopher Epictetus (c. 50–135 CE) shared five powerful ideas on this score that have stood the test of time. I call these five timeless ideas the CEO Playbook.

Write these five ideas down. Read them daily. Live the CEO Playbook daily!

THE CEO PLAYBOOK

1. **"First say to yourself what you would be; and then do what you have to do."**[3]

   Translation: Figure out what kind of contribution you want to make…and then do what you must do to become the kind of person who consistently makes that contribution. Live the vision of your dreams!

2. **"Seek not the good in external things; seek it in yourself."**[4]

   Translation: Take relentless action for the sake of doing the right thing—by making a contribution that is the best and highest one you can make. Do not seek the praise of other people.

3. **"There is only one way to happiness and that is to cease worrying about things which are beyond the power of our will."**[5]

Translation: If you have no control over a situation, stop worrying about it. On the other hand, if you *do* have control over a situation, as both Lisa, Carol, and I did, see #2. And remember: You *always* have control over your thoughts. Shift your thinking in productive ways to focus on what you *can* do.

4. **"Any person capable of angering you becomes your master; he can anger you only when you permit yourself to be disturbed by him."**[6]

Translation: Learn to act independently and set your own course, without being bullied, controlled, or manipulated by others. When people do you wrong, learn to let go of the anger—otherwise you are giving your power away and staying a victim.

5. **"It's not what happens to you, but how you react to it that matters."**[7]

Translation: Don't react. Respond. *Choose* your response. The greatest luxury and the greatest necessity in life is choice.

What stops us from reclaiming agency and autonomy in our lives? From claiming the seat at the table that we deserve? There are ten thousand possible answers, but in reality there is only one correct answer: fear.

DO THIS

Read and live by the CEO Playbook I have shared with you in this chapter. If you do that, you will have the toolkit you need when the time comes to move beyond fear and reclaim the leadership God meant you to have in your own life. Letting anyone else assume that leadership is a dangerous business indeed.

Thank God for the abundance He has promised. It is God's will that we should have an abundant life in all things. When we reclaim our agency, we do that so that we can help Him to help us.

8. BEFORE YOU MOVE ON TO THE THIRD COMMANDMENT, DO THIS

QUESTIONS: COMMANDMENT II

- Have you written out and posted, in a place you can see them each and every day, your CEO Playbook? If not, please do this before you move on to the next commandment.

- What was the last major obstacle you faced? How were you curious about it? How could you have been curious about it? What did you or can you learn from it?

- What's a recent example of how you defined yourself by your victories rather than your defeats?

- Are you still taking personal private time—time to just be quiet, all by yourself—each day? (If not, please re-engage with this commitment before you move on to the next commandment. This is how you build up the Courage to Hear, the Courage to Dream Big, and the Courage to Do the Right Thing.)

ACTIONS: COMMANDMENT II

- Identify what being CEO of You looks and feels like for you. Find what makes you feel more empowered, more in control, and more enlightened. Schedule time for those things in your day.

- List the top 25 things you've ever imagined that you wanted to do with your life. Next, boil that list down to 5 items, and set the others aside for now. When you have conquered your top 5 items, you can revisit the longer list. For now, get to work on this "Focus 5" list! Plan your day with your Focus 5 list in mind. Make a commitment to take some kind of action on each of the items on that list each day, no matter how small the contribution may seem.

- Take responsibility for your results. Resolve to learn from your mistakes and not repeat them. Learn to forgive yourself and let go. Find joy in accepting yourself as the CEO of You.

Once you have done all this, you will be ready to move on to Commandment III.

COMMANDMENT III

Break the Addiction to Fear

ESCAPE

"I have not ceased being fearful, but I have ceased to let fear control me."

— *Erica Jong*

9. THE FIVE QUESTIONS

"Ultimately, nothing in life is to be feared, it is only to be understood. Now is the time to understand more, so that we may fear less."

— *Marie Curie*

Fear plagues everyone…but it doesn't need to control everyone. In my middle school years, I played basketball, and I was pretty good. I never had formal lessons. I never attended sports camps. I was not trained by coaches. I just played with other kids at the local playgrounds and at school.

When I arrived at a new school called Longmeadow, I decided to try out for the team, and I made it…but the joy I felt at having achieved that was quickly paired up with a very different set of emotions. I was flooded with insecurity. The girls who were now my teammates spoke enthusiastically of the summer basketball camps, drills, and fitness coaches who had helped them to hone their skills on the court. I knew I had none of these.

What I had was grit, determination, competitiveness, a whole lot of playground experience, a love for the game, and a height advantage. But as the season began, I wasn't really sure those would be enough to see me through.

There was one point guard in particular who stood out. Nancy had an amazing shot; she led the offense. She talked all the time about what she had learned and practiced at summer basketball camps. She wasn't bragging; this was just the norm for her and for others. I couldn't help wondering: *Would I ever really be able to play at Nancy's level? Were my natural talent and my height enough? Could I really expect to compete on the same level as all the other girls who had made it onto this team? Could I possibly be as good as they were without the support and formal training they had received? Or would I always be a few levels below players like Nancy—people who "really knew" what they were doing?*

I was focusing on other people and comparing myself to them, as opposed to focusing on what *I* could contribute. I was using the fact that I had had a *different* set of experiences from the others to support the idea that I had had a *lesser* set of experiences. This is a debilitating pattern of thinking that disproportionately affects women and people of color in all walks of life.

I didn't realize it at the time, but my assessment of my own abilities and experiences was way off. I had a lot to contribute, and I had accumulated plenty of experiences that other people on the team did not have!

Sidenote: I believe we all need to learn to celebrate differences. The majority experience is not necessarily better than a more unique set of experiences just because it is the more common one. We celebrate Bill Gates and Mark Zuckerberg for their accomplishments, even though they did not complete college. So does it really make sense to automatically consider others deficient if they don't have a college degree?

Our differences make us unique, not less than. Our work environments must not be designed to diminish people who haven't followed some expected cultural norm. And we certainly must not diminish ourselves!

> Our differences make us unique, not less than. Our work environments must not be designed to diminish people who haven't followed some expected cultural norm. And we certainly must not diminish ourselves!

With the support and guidance of my basketball coach, I overcame my limiting beliefs about my lack of experience and my ability to contribute. The particular strategy she used was to pose five powerful questions—questions that stuck with me:

- Where is this fear really coming from?

  › It was coming from a set of inaccurate and impractical beliefs about who I was and what I was capable of.

- What is my desired outcome in this situation?

  › I wanted to become the best basketball player I was capable of becoming, and I wanted to make a contribution to the team.

- Does this fear serve or undermine that outcome?

  › It undermined it. It did not serve the outcomes I wanted.

- What's the worst that could happen if I do this?

  › I might not make the team.

- Is there anything I can do to keep that worst-case scenario from happening?

  ❯ Yes, I could ask the coach for suggestions about where I needed to improve—and then work my tail off. I had grit and determination. I had a strong work ethic and knew I could, would, and had to work harder.

DO THIS

Learn and practice asking yourself these questions:

➡ Where is this fear really coming from?

➡ What is my desired outcome in this situation?

➡ Does this fear serve or undermine that outcome?

➡ What's the worst that could happen if I do this?

➡ Is there anything I can do to keep that worst-case scenario from happening?

After talking to my coach, I opted to move out of my comfort zone—by putting myself out there and focusing on my strengths. Before long, I realized that these strengths tended toward defense and that they could indeed be important to our season—basketball camp or no basketball camp. I won the starting job as center, and as the season progressed, I became a more and more accomplished defensive player. My confidence grew with every game, and I was able to make some important contributions on the court. I finally felt like part of the team.

Then came the day we played a school I'll call Wilson Academy.

Wilson Academy fielded an all-white team. During our game with them, a couple of the girls on the Wilson team thought it would be funny to start making racist slurs, up to and including the N-word.

They were relentless. I was their entertainment for this game. Their abuse got to me, and I lost my focus—which, looking back, I realize was their intent: to make sure I had a bad defensive game.

I did.

That night, I went home angry with myself for letting the taunts get to me and for disappointing myself and my teammates. I thought about quitting. My spirit was hurting; I had done nothing to these girls. I would never treat someone like that. I had shown up with my teammates to compete fair and square…but that day, they beat me.

I called my mom in tears. I told her I was going to quit playing basketball. Here was my reasoning: I had let everyone down—not just myself, but also my coach and the rest of the team. If I was going to be a liability, which clearly I had been, I felt I had no business walking out onto the court.

My fear this time was different. What if it happened again? What if I was so easily rattled by an opposing player—any opposing player—that I ended up hurting the team? What if I couldn't execute in the way the coach expected? This, by the way, was perfectionism, another classic symptom of an addiction to fear. It's the fear that we can't do it all, or can't do it perfectly, every time.

> Perfectionism means you say "no" to moving forward on something important because you are afraid that you can't guarantee an absolutely optimal result every single time.

Of course, there is a time for caution, and there is a time for quality control, and yes, there is a time for high standards to be set and met. But if you find you are *consistently* turning your back on opportunities to grow as a person because you are holding yourself to a level of performance that no one could realistically be expected to hit, you may want to examine the possibility that you are looking for reasons to close doors, rather than open them, and that you are looking for validation from the outside, rather than from the inside. And these are classic symptoms of fear addiction.

We feed our fears and ultimately paralyze ourselves when we get into the habit of saying "no" because we can't promise absolute freedom from error. In these situations, we are staying within our comfort zone and deepening our addiction to fear. We need to remind ourselves that it is okay to get more information before we make a decision, it is okay to ask for help, and it is okay to move forward.

Move past mistakes and blunders. They are over. Let them go. I know—it's easier said than done. But you must do it anyway.

There was a long silence as I waited to hear how my mom would respond to my declaration that I would be leaving the team. I think she knew I wanted to hear her response to my "decision." (In fact, I wasn't going to make any decision without hearing what she thought about it, but as a teenager I certainly wasn't going to admit that.)

The silence lasted for a long time. Eventually, my mom said, "If you quit, then you will have lost, and they will have won. If you quit, you will let them deprive you of something you enjoy. Losing the game is one thing. Walking away is a far worse thing to do to your teammates, and to yourself, than losing a single game. Think about it. There will be another game. But if you quit the team, you will not just be letting down your teammates; you will be losing the battle of life. Letting your fears and failures interrupt your plans is the very worst kind of losing. *No one ever said it would be easy.* But you can't let fear stop you. You just can't. There will be more challenges ahead, and there will be failure too, but you simply cannot let those girls win. You will find a way. You will stand up and push through. Now get some rest. It will be better in the morning."

> No one ever said it would be easy.

Her suggestion that things would be better in the morning sounded like nonsense to me, but I did as she said.

She was right. It *was* better in the morning. The next day, I began asking myself those same questions:

- Where is this fear really coming from?

  > It was coming from a desire to meet an impossible standard and perhaps also from a desire to hide any evidence that I was not perfect.

- What is my desired outcome in this situation?

  > I still wanted to become the best basketball player I was capable of becoming, and I still wanted to make a contribution to the team.

- Does this fear serve or undermine that outcome?

  > It undermined it. It would not only undermine the outcome I wanted; it would undermine me as a person.

- What's the worst that could happen if I do this?

  > I might not get my shot back, but even if that turned out to be the case, I could still help and support the team in other ways.

- Is there something I can do to keep that worst-case scenario from happening?

  > Yes. I could practice more and play more, which would increase the odds that I would be able to perform at the top of my abilities the next time I found myself in a stressful situation.

I stayed on the team. Had I not, I would be regretting it to this very day.

My mother was right, by the way. There was plenty of pain, hurt, and failure ahead. But I am still standing and still pushing through.

This is what we must all learn to do. Take a close look at our fears. Set the irrational ones aside. Push through. Brush our knees off. Get back up and get back in the game. Live without regret.

10. THE ESSENTIAL SELF

"Understand: we are all too afraid—of offending people, of stirring up conflict, of standing out from the crowd, of taking bold action. For thousands of years, our relationship to this emotion has evolved—from a primitive fear of nature, to generalized anxiety about the future, to the fearful attitude that now dominates us. As rational, productive adults, we are called upon to finally overcome this downward trend and to evolve beyond our fears."

— *Robert Greene*

Make no mistake: fear is natural. It is part of the human toolkit. It has a purpose, and we are each blessed to have it. Fear can serve as a warning, a critical part of our defense system, a powerful emotion that can alert us to dangers and difficulties that may emerge and are best avoided. Without that warning system, our lives would be shorter, more painful, and more brutal. When fear is constructive, it helps us to identify *major* threats and *genuine* emergencies. But fear is much, much more than a flashing red light.

Sometimes fear points us toward something we need to avoid. But sometimes, upon deeper examination, we realize that fear points us toward a new possibility, a new chance to grow, a new opportunity to expand our capabilities by moving past what is comfortable and familiar. If we learn to *listen* to fear, if we learn to use it constructively, we will find that it often directs us toward new opportunity. The key to determining whether we are looking at a genuine danger or an opportunity for growth lies in our ability to ask ourselves those questions I have already shared with you:

- Where is this fear really coming from?
- What is my desired outcome in this situation?
- Does this fear serve or undermine that outcome?
- What's the worst that could happen if I do this?
- Is there anything I can do to keep that worst-case scenario from happening?

These questions help us figure out whether we are really looking at a dangerous situation…or at a door that's worth learning how to open. They enable us to *harness* fear and use it to our advantage. If we step back and examine our fears closely, we will often find that they are pointing us toward new people who are worth meeting, new experiences that are worth having, and new challenges that are worth taking on.

"First we must unflinchingly face our fears and honestly ask ourselves, *why are we afraid?* This confrontation will, to some measure, grant us power. We shall never be cured of fear by escapism or repression, for the more we attempt

> to ignore and repress our fears, the more we multiply our inner conflicts… By looking squarely and honestly at our fears we learn that many of them reside in some childhood need or apprehension… By bringing our fears to the forefront of consciousness, we may find them to be more imaginary than real."
>
> —Martin Luther King, Jr.

We must *respect* our fears enough to acknowledge and examine them carefully, but we must never, ever make the mistake of allowing our fears to govern our life. An addiction to fear paralyzes us and robs us of the potential to learn, grow, and contribute. If we are serious about breaking the addiction—if we are serious about refusing to sign our lives over to fear—we will acquire the essential skill of breaking the bonds of our addiction…by posing those five powerful questions and then making a conscious choice to set unjustified fears aside. Breaking an addiction to fear is not a one-time event. It is part of the human condition. It is a constant battle, and it is not always easy. But it is a battle worth fighting. You cannot live the life you are meant to live if you are addicted to fear.

There is no crime in *noticing* an addiction to fear. But it *is* wrong to notice the signs of this addiction and, as an adult, choose to stay within your comfort zone. Use the questions I have shared with you to start a conversation with yourself that moves you beyond your comfort zone! Look at, and be ready to answer, the powerful sub-questions each main question points toward:

- Where is this fear really coming from?

  › Am I choosing to compare myself to others, rather than looking at what I can contribute? How is that limiting me?

  › Am I holding myself to the standard of being perfect, of executing at a level of total quality, every single time? How is that limiting me?

- What is my desired outcome in this situation?

  › What do I want to be, do, become, or contribute right now?

  › What do I want to make happen?

- Does this fear serve or undermine that commitment?

  › If I set aside this fear and take action, what is the upside?

  › If I listen to this fear and let it determine my actions, what is the downside? What will that decision cost me?

- What's the worst that could happen if I do this?

  › Is the worst-case scenario I am envisioning really accurate?

  › Is it really all that bad?

  › How do I know?

- Is there something I can do to keep that worst-case scenario from happening?

  › What action or actions could I take to improve the potential downside?

  › What new approach could I try?

  › What untapped or emerging skills could I refine?

  › Who else could I work with?

(For a downloadable "Breaking the Addiction to Fear" worksheet that you can use any time you are feeling immobilized by fear, visit couragebydesign.com.)

By asking and answering these questions for ourselves, we can break our cycle of addiction to fear. Ultimately, it is up to us whether we step back from our instinctive responses and assess these issues for ourselves.

When you feel fearful, learn to call a time-out and listen to your best self. Remember, this is all about choices. Courage really is a choice… and it requires you to make the conscious decision to step back from fears that do not support the best possible version of you. Tell the fear, "I'll have to get back to you later."

DO THIS

When you feel fearful, learn to call a time-out and listen to your best self. Choose to step back from fears that do not support the best possible version of you. Tell the irrational fear, "I'll have to get back to you later."

Practice building up the Courage to Hear. What does your inner voice, the voice of the most authentic YOU deep inside, tell you to do when a fear stops you cold? Shelly Francis, author of *The Courage Way*, puts this same question in words that have come to mean a lot to me and that can guide us all past the easy but costly reactions that can strengthen an addiction to fear:

"Our basic premise is that inside of each person is the essential self who continues to grow and yet somehow, deep down, remains constant. Every person has access to this inner source of truth, named in various wisdom traditions as identity and integrity, inner teacher, heart, inner compass, spirit, or soul. Your true self is a source of guidance and strength that helps you find your way through life's complexities and challenges. When you begin to listen to and trust the truest part of yourself, your choices and relationships flow from that trust, begetting more trust."

—Shelly Francis

What Francis is describing is how some of the greatest figures from human history—people like Helen Keller, Mahatma Gandhi, and Dr. Martin Luther King, Jr.—learned to overcome the all-too-common habit of letting fear dictate their choices. All of them, of course, faced deeply fearful situations. Keller experienced a terrifying illness that left her deaf and blind in childhood. Gandhi faced the daunting legal, political, and financial resources of the British Empire, all of which were arrayed against him or anyone else who dared to advocate for the independence of India. King received countless death threats from people who were troubled by his work to secure civil rights for African Americans. Yet all of them learned to take time out to listen to their "essential self," and all of them learned to turn away from fears that did not support the best possible version of themselves.

Breaking a fear addiction is not easy. Consider, though, that countless others have struggled with this same challenge, and countless others have broken the bonds of fear by learning to tune in to their truest, deepest self when they felt fearful. Remembering this, and following their example, can help take some of the pressure off.

11. BEFORE YOU MOVE ON TO THE FOURTH COMMANDMENT, DO THIS

QUESTIONS: COMMANDMENT III

- Take the time to review the powerful questions below. What is a situation you could apply them to right now?

  > Where is this fear really coming from?

  > What is my desired outcome in this situation?

  > Does this fear serve or undermine that outcome?

  > What's the worst that could happen if I do this?

  > Is there anything I can do to keep that worst-case scenario from happening?

- Who is your personal hero when it comes to overcoming an addiction to fear? Why that person?

- What are your recurrent fears and crises—the emotionally driven shutdowns that typically keep you from being your best self? Identify at least three.

- Are you still taking personal private time—time just to be quiet, all by yourself—each day? If not, please re-engage with this commitment before you move on to the next commandment. This is how you build up the Courage to Hear, the Courage to Dream Big, and the Courage to Do the Right Thing.

ACTIONS: COMMANDMENT III

- Find a picture of your hero in the area of personal courage. Put the picture someplace you can see it every day.
- Lean into your courage and away from your fear AT LEAST ONCE today. Say *Yes* to something you would ordinarily have said *No* to. Or have the courage to say *No* to something that doesn't serve you.
- Download and use the free "Breaking the Addiction to Fear" tool (at couragebydesign.com).

Once you have done all this, you will be ready to move on to Commandment IV.

COMMANDMENT IV

Harness the Power of Faith

BELIEVE

"If you lose faith, you lose all."

— *Eleanor Roosevelt*

12. THE FAITHFUL EXECUTIVE

> "It is not the strength of the body that counts,
> but the strength of the spirit."
> —J. R. R. Tolkien

Two things my mother said to me following that episode at Wilson Academy resonated powerfully through my life from that moment on: "No one said it would be easy" and "Find a way."

There had been a note of assurance and optimism in my mother's voice as she said these words, a tone that let me know, at the deepest possible level, that if I quit that basketball team, I would be choosing a path that was not meant for me. Those words made me step back, take a deep breath, and connect with something bigger than myself. In those two simple phrases, my mother had given me a great gift: the ability to harness, at a practical level, the life-changing power of faith.

Faith is the belief that you can and will find a way to fulfill your purpose in life as you understand that purpose…the belief that you are *meant* to find a way…and the belief that you have the right, the ability, and the duty to do this.

When you have faith, you stop making excuses and stop

playing games. You believe you have everything you need to find your way right now. And you take action.

The phrase "No one said it would be easy" gave me the capacity to put what I had been going through in perspective. Those words let me see the obstacle in front of me as a temporary setback, not as a permanent barrier to becoming the person I was meant to be.

The words "Find a way" gave me hope for the future. As I thought about those words and the challenge I faced, I knew that with help from my Creator, I had found my way past countless challenges before. With that same help, I could find my way again. I could start to dream with confidence again.

That confidence has another name: faith.

Those two simple sentences of my mother's lifted me up, and the force that did the lifting was faith. This was her gift to me: a deep, abiding faith—a certainty—that I would indeed be able to find a source of resilience in response to the racism I had encountered. Those two life-changing sentences of hers, along with her assurance that God would not give me more than I could handle, awakened me to the practical, everyday power of faith and to the decision to harness that power every day of my life.

The understanding of faith that I just shared with you is something I coach people in all walks of life to come back to constantly, to ground themselves in. Faith is the foundation, the rock upon which we can build our lives. It is the best starting point for every decision. It is the path traveled by the special person I call the *faithful executive.*

This role of faithful executive is one you will want to take on, whether or not others think of you as an executive and whether or not you lead a team. Remember: execution simply means taking action, and that is what executives do—they act.

When you are a faithful executive, taking action in a faithful manner—finding a way—is your reason for getting up in the morning. Taking action faithfully is a way of returning yourself, as often and as purposefully as necessary, to your foundation. It is a way of connecting and reconnecting to those two powerful sentences that can instantly latch you onto something larger than yourself:

- *No one said it would be easy.*
- *Find a way.*

When you are a faithful executive, you have discovered your reason for being, and you use the gifts and talents you have been blessed with to serve others and fulfill your purpose in life—regardless of any obstacles that present themselves. You do not complain, even under the worst of circumstances. There is no room in the life of a faithful executive for self-pity, for finger-pointing, or for excuses. There is only accountability.

You know you are going to encounter circumstances that challenge you from time to time. You also know that you are on a mission and that God does not give you more than you can handle. When things get tough, you don't let yourself off the hook. You continue to pursue your mission in life. You continue to live your values. You continue to move forward. You remind yourself as often as necessary that no one said it would be easy. And you find a way.

A faithful executive is not necessarily someone who leads a team or an organization. It is someone who accepts the truth that *no one said it would be easy,* someone who commits to *finding a way,* someone who takes action. A faithful executive focuses on what they will do, not on what they can't or won't do.

One incident in particular pointed me irrevocably toward the path of the faithful executive. As fate would have it, it was another conversation with my mother.

13. WHERE DO YOU NEED TO GO?

"Let your faith be bigger than your fear."

—*Anonymous*

People often ask me how and why I made the decision to leave my corporate job to launch my own business. Why would I trade a secure job with benefits and a salary—and plenty of perks like first-class business travel—to take what many people in my world considered a major—and inexcusable—gamble?

I can tell you that this was not an impetuous decision, nor was it made easily. I made it in response to a question I kept asking myself, a question I could not avoid: *Is this really where I need to go next in my life?*

The week I finally came up with an answer to that question, I was finishing a 30-day-straight work stint at a prestigious advertising agency where I had been working for the past two years. During this period, I had had no days off, and each of those working days had been a long one, with plenty of evenings and late nights spent in the agency's venerable, but lonely, offices. I was the only agency employee in the building after hours. I was working hard on a client's business, doing all I could to maximize the value we delivered to that client. The sheer amount of time I was devoting to this client's project was staggering. As I began to look at my situation, it occurred to me that the risk might not be in leaving my "safe" job at that agency but rather in staying.

For one thing, my health was definitely suffering—I had recurring fibroids in spite of my young age, and I had undergone multiple surgeries for that. On top of that problem, long hours, stress, fear, worry, and a perpetual lack of sleep all contributed to a series of concerning health issues. Adding to the stress I felt was a long list of challenges connected to being a woman, and a person of color, in an industry that had long been dominated by white men.

Knowing that I had to work twice as hard to be taken half as seriously was taking a toll on me, as were the sexist attitudes of some of my colleagues. One of them had actually posted a Playboy centerfold on a wall in our office and attached a sticky note that read: "Dee, is this you?" Somehow people thought this was okay, and even amusing. No one objected. I had to take it down. This was long before the #MeToo movement, of course. That incident was not an isolated one. Suffice to say, I was not happy at work.

Contributing to this unhappiness—and even more concerning to me than the attitudes of my coworkers—was the real question of financial achievement. This was important to me. The reality that I was not earning what I was worth had become increasingly impossible for me to ignore. When I calculated what I was actually bringing in, I concluded that if I factored in all of the hours I was working, that generous salary I was earning at the ad agency was no longer quite so generous. In fact, dividing the salary by the hours I worked showed that I was making what I could have made working in a fast-food restaurant or in a retail establishment! It was dangerously close to minimum wage!

Was this really my path—to work that hard, for that pathetic return, and all for someone else? Was this really where I wanted to be going in my life?

I had done some research on my own about financial freedom. I had read (*devoured* would be a better word) several books on this subject. When I don't know something, I turn to books! As a result of all my reading, I had determined that financial independence was my goal. And it was increasingly clear to me that my job at the agency was not going to be the means to such an end. As someone who grew up without real financial security, the prospect of working hard but *not* obtaining financial freedom horrified me. I was deeply hungry for that freedom. Faith, when combined with that kind of hunger, has a way of overpowering fear.

One night, when I was working until nearly midnight at the agency's office, my path became clear to me. I saw that I was giving up way too much in order to do what I was doing. The long hours and the stress of the job were taking a toll on my physical and emotional well-being. So were the attitudes of my coworkers toward me as a woman of color. I knew I had to re-evaluate my plan and start thinking more strategically about where I wanted to go in my life.

Over the course of the next few weeks, I paid very close attention to those around me and above me (hierarchically speaking) at the agency I worked for. I noticed something I had either not noticed before or chosen not to notice: *I did not see many females of color anywhere in the executive ranks of the organization.*

I already knew that I personally did not receive much encouragement from colleagues and superiors about the prospect of becoming an executive at the agency. But the lack of women of color in anything remotely resembling an executive career track got me thinking. A little voice inside me started asking questions—questions I couldn't ignore: *How much opportunity would there really be for me until I hit the proverbial glass ceiling? And what then? Was I even appreciated for all of my hard work and dedication? What was I doing? Why was I giving up so much? Was I selling myself short? If I was going to put so many hours and so much effort into someone's business, shouldn't it be my own?*

When I listened to the little voice, I knew I was not performing at the level I was capable of. I knew I could do more. I knew I *had* to do more if I was going to be true to myself. I did not want someone else to be in control of my future.

That little voice inside me told me that it was time for me to start my own business. I decided to listen to it.

There is a little voice inside all of us that points us toward the true path, the path we are meant to follow, the path that invites us to move past our comfort zone, trust our instincts, and become who we are meant to be. It is all too easy to drown that voice out. It takes courage to listen to that voice and follow it. Faith gives us that courage. I call faith the *Courage to Hear*.

The first person I told about my decision was my mother. This was a major moment for both of us because I knew full well that her preference would have been for me to stay with the "safe" job I had at the advertising agency. For her, having grown up in and around situations of deep economic challenge, getting that job at the agency was the *reason* I had worked so hard for so many years. Why walk away from stability?

To her credit, though, as my mother listened to me explain what had gone into my decision, she came to understand that I had reached a point in my life where I had to make my own choices. That, of course, was the kind of life she wanted me to lead: one where I was pursuing what was most important to me as a person. So when I told her what I had in mind and why it was so important to me, she took a deep breath, looked me in the eye, and told me that it wasn't the decision she would make but that she would support me, whatever I did.

Tears came to both our eyes when she said that. And then I heard those extraordinary words from her once again:

"I guess you know it's not going to be easy, honey," she said, "but no one ever *said* it would be easy. You will find a way."

Those words lifted me up all over again, just like they had when I was contemplating quitting the basketball team. Only this time, I wasn't walking away from my dream; I was striding toward it, and my mother knew that. As she gave me her blessing, I knew that she knew I had found my own path and that I had the faith necessary to follow it, wherever it led. For years, she had taught me to rely on God—but she had taught me also to take action and to remember that our time on earth is precious and limited. As I hugged her, I remembered something else she had been telling me for years: "You have to help God help you!" We have to do our part. This principle still guides me. Are you doing your part? Are you helping Him help you? He lives up to His promise.

Being a faithful executive means having the courage to make choices and take actions that allow you to live your own life fully, with no regrets, starting right now, no matter where you are—because you know that time is both fleeting and precious. It means remembering that *your job is to help God help you!*

"IF YOU CAN RECLAIM YOUR TALENT, YOU CAN RECLAIM YOUR LIFE"

On August 10, 1991, a late-night fight broke out at a gathering outside of Louie's Texas Red Hots restaurant at the intersection of East Delevan and Bailey Avenue in Buffalo, NY. In the ensuing mayhem, Torriano Jackson was shot and killed. Based on an anonymous tip, the police arrested Valentino Dixon for his murder and for shooting at three other people.

Just two days after Valentino's arrest, Lamarr Scott confessed to the news media that he had in fact shot and killed Jackson. Despite this confession, Scott was not taken into custody, and detectives continued to pursue Valentino. Prosecutors then built a case against Valentino based on several shaky eyewitnesses (some of whom later recanted and claimed to have been pressured by the police to frame Valentino). At trial, Valentino was convicted and sentenced to 38 1/2 years-to-life in prison.

Valentino struggled to adjust to life in prison—until he reconnected with his inner passion for art. He regained his motivation to draw by following his uncle's advice: "if you reclaim your talent, you can reclaim your life." Valentino has been drawing ever since; for more than two decades, he drew from six to ten hours a day.

At one point, the warden at Attica Correctional Facility asked Valentino to draw the 12th hole of the legendary Augusta National Golf Club. Valentino, who had never set foot on a golf course and knew nothing about the sport, started drawing images inspired by photos in the magazine *Golf Digest*. Eventually, Valentino even drew his own golf creations and said that golf art became his escape from the harsh reality of prison.

In 2012, *Golf Digest* editorial director Max Adler featured Valentino and his stunning artwork in a "Golf Saved My Life" column. ...On September 19, 2018—27 years after Valentino Dixon's initial wrongful conviction—Lamarr Scott pleaded guilty to the murder of Torriano Jackson, and Valentino walked out of prison a free man.[8]

It was my honor and my privilege to interview Valentino Dixon for this book. Here is what he had to say on the topic of making choices and taking actions that allow us to live our life fully:

My uncle told me that if I could reclaim my talent, I could reclaim my life, and honestly I think that is something that is true for everyone, no matter what their situation happens to be. In my case, the situation was wrongful conviction and incarceration, even though I had eight witnesses and a confession clearing me. I was blessed, though, because while I was in prison, my uncle told me the truth about what the right response to my situation was. He said, "You remember how you used to love drawing? You may have to draw yourself out of prison." By that point all my appeals had been exhausted, and I hadn't drawn or painted in seven years.

But I decided to follow my uncle's advice. That decision of mine eventually led to the drawing of the 12th hole at Augusta, which led to the feature in Golf Digest, which led to a documentary about my case, which eventually led to my release. My uncle was absolutely right. The only way out was for me to draw my way out. But first, I had to make the decision to take action.

There were two parts to that decision for me: I had to strengthen my faith in my Creator, which was dormant when I landed in prison. And I had to do something daily to put my talent to use again and develop it, because that was dormant too. I woke both of those things up while I was in prison. And I'm still striving to keep them awake to this day.

14. FAITH IS TAKING ACTION

"Faith is taking the first step, even when you don't see the whole staircase."

— *Martin Luther King, Jr.*

I consider faith a non-negotiable part of the journey toward a courageous life, but I don't pretend that any individual's faith can be determined or dictated by someone else. I take a pragmatic approach to faith. I see it as the fuel that moves you forward with courage in pursuit of the person you know you are meant to be. I see faith as the willingness and the bravery to ask yourself:

What is my true path? Am I on that path? If not…

What am I sacrificing, not just financially but in terms of my health, my family life, and my sense of self by not following my true path?

What am I sacrificing by not listening to my inner voice, by not doing the work I was born to do?

And is that a price I am willing to pay?

I believe faith is the readiness to cultivate the Courage to Hear—and then change what you are doing so you can pursue, with certainty, the path you are meant to follow. Every other aspect of the faith experience, in my view, is a matter of individual choice. But I believe we all have an obligation to ask ourselves whether we are on the path our Higher Power is pointing us toward.

So if you are in a state of stress, anxiety, and exhaustion all the time—as I was when I was working at that advertising agency—that's a sign that something is not working and you need to make a change. Having faith means noticing that need, recognizing when you are on the wrong path. Having faith means listening to the voice that tells you it is time to pursue your true calling. Having faith means stepping out of your comfort zone and finding the best possible way to make a change, even if doing so is not likely to be easy.

Faith is, in short, about taking action. It is not merely something you verbalize. It is leaving situations that don't support the contribution you are meant to make in life—and finding, or creating, situations that do.

For me, faith was resigning from a job that I knew, deep down, was not right for me. It was the courage to leave a marriage. It was the resolve to find new ways to move forward after failures. What is it for you?

> ## DO THIS
>
> Ask yourself: *What needs to change in my life right now for me to follow the path I was born to follow? What is getting in the way? What is the single most important change that has to happen? What action will I take to make that change?*

My challenge to you now is to harness the power of faith in your life on a practical level. Make faith your strategy for awakening courage at the moments you need it most so that you can find a way to act on your purpose. Commit to becoming a faithful executive—and to taking action.

Faith simply means trust in action—learning to trust yourself and your path enough to pursue it fiercely. It is something you can do if you are a Christian, a Buddhist, a Muslim, a Jew, or a member of any other faith system—or no system at all. This is not a question of theology. It is a question of choosing to claim agency in your life by defining and summoning your own Higher Power. Not anyone else's—yours.

There came a point in my life, shortly after reading Deepak Chopra's book *The Seven Spiritual Laws of Success,* when I realized that pursuing my calling really was a matter of faith. That pursuit touched all other aspects of my life. In particular, I learned that when someone does me wrong—by posting a rude photograph and an insulting note in a public place, for instance—that's God's business, not mine. I learned to let go and let the universe take care of it. That is the courage of forgiveness. That is the courage of faith.

From Chopra I also learned that life is, ultimately, about giving. When you focus on giving back, on contributing, on gratefully receiving gifts and keeping them circulating with full faith that the universe will take care of you and guide you, then the universe keeps you on the right path.

I found deep solace in recognizing that the universe plays a role in achievement and fulfillment and that this shifted attitude can be used as a foundation for living my best life—if I summon the Courage to Hear my own inner voice.

We each face the challenge of developing a deep, abiding trust in the awesome, transformative power of pursuing our own purpose. We each have a right and a duty to listen to our inner voice, to live in accordance with the proposition that we are here for a reason. The clearer we are about what that reason is, what our purpose is, and what the way forward looks like for us, the better off we will be. And once we learn to seize the moment by trusting and acting on that little voice we hear, we will find that powerful forces come to our aid. I'll share how that happened for me in the next commandment.

15. BEFORE YOU MOVE ON TO THE FIFTH COMMANDMENT, DO THIS

QUESTIONS: COMMANDMENT IV

- How do you define your own Higher Power? Not anyone else's...yours.

- Think of someone who has done you wrong. Are you willing to let go of that hurt and let the universe handle what happens to the person or people responsible? Why or why not? What would it take for you to make the choice to do that?

- Are you still taking personal private time—time just to be quiet, all by yourself—each day? If not, please re-engage with this commitment before you move on to the next commandment. This is how you build up the Courage to Hear, the Courage to Dream Big, and the Courage to Do the Right Thing.

ACTIONS: COMMANDMENT IV

- Address a current challenge in your life by cultivating the Courage to Hear the little voice inside telling you what the right next step is. Hear that voice that is usually drowned out. This is one of your many superpowers. Remember, it can be exercised only in moments of stillness.

- You've certainly heard the expression "hiding your light under a bushel." It means ignoring or obscuring a talent or gift you possess and could be sharing with others. What is a light in *your* life that could be shining more brightly for others?

- Find a way to use that talent or gift in a way that serves other people. Take a moment to reflect on the joy you experience when you do this.

Once you have done all this, you will be ready to move on to Commandment V.

COMMANDMENT V

Find Your Calling

MISSION MATTERS!

"When you find your WHY, you don't hit snooze no more!"

— *Eric Thomas*

16. YOUR BIG "WHY"

"The whole point of being alive is to become the person you were intended to be, to grow out of and into yourself again and again. I believe you can do this only when you stop long enough to hear the whisper you might have drowned out, that small voice compelling you toward your calling."

— *Oprah Winfrey*

I told you a little earlier how my mother accepted and embraced my decision to leave a "safe" corporate job, even though we both knew that she did not want me to do that. So here's a question: *Why* did she support me?

I believe my mother stood by me for a simple reason: she realized that I knew, with absolute certainty, that staying in that job at the ad agency was not what I was meant to do with my life—that I had another calling I had to pursue.

When I talk about following your calling in life, I'm talking about what some people refer to as a "purpose" and what other people refer to as the "big why." I prefer the word "calling" over the other terms, because for me, it evokes the idea of being summoned, persistently and patiently, by something larger than ourselves. What is summoning us, exactly? The chance to be, do, contribute, and become what we are meant to. Pursuing this calling is what makes us who we are.

The words we use to describe our calling may change with the passage of time, but the calling itself is always there, always waiting for us, always offering us the chance to live the fullest possible life. So, what we think of as our "purpose" may change over time, and the "why" that we identify for taking a certain course of action may shift as the years go by. Yet that which calls us in the right direction *continues* to call us in the right direction, no matter what happens to us, no matter how many obstacles we may encounter.

> If we are brave enough to heed our calling when it summons us, the direction in which we should be pointing our lives becomes clearer and clearer over time.

This commandment is about identifying and acting on your true calling in life. I can't overemphasize the importance of this subject. The only way for me to get across to you what I have learned about it is to explain how my own calling has become clearer and clearer to me as I have pursued it…and also to share some of the ways I took action on it. I've come to discover that the clarity of your calling is connected to the quality of the *intention* with which you pursue it. That's the thing about a calling: the more intentionally you pursue it, the clearer its expression becomes to you.

My calling in life is to leave people and places better than I found them.

That's my calling. It's the foundation of everything I do. What's yours?

Before you complete this commandment, you'll know.

17. WHO ARE YOUR CALLING ALLIES?

"Love your calling with passion.
It is the meaning of your life."

—Auguste Rodin

My very first memory of pursuing my calling comes from when I was 12 years old. It involves two "calling allies," two people who were willing to help me identify who I was meant to be—willing to help me summon the courage necessary to navigate toward becoming that person.

> **DO THIS**
>
> Be open to the coaching of "calling allies"—people who are willing to help you identify who you are meant to be, and to help you summon the courage necessary to navigate the path toward becoming that person.

Back when I was 12, I didn't have much pocket money, and I wanted some. Things were tight financially around our house, and my mother didn't have any room in the family budget to hand out much of an allowance. So, like a lot of budding entrepreneurs, I started looking for ways to get myself some additional income.

I came across what sounded to me like an opportunity, and one night, when my mom came back from working one of her long shifts, I told her about it. I said, "Mom, Mrs. Henry said she's looking for someone who can clean house for her. She said she'd pay me five dollars if I do it this Saturday, but I have to get your permission. Can I tell her yes?" (Mrs. Henry was my piano teacher.)

My mom looked at me across the kitchen table for a long moment. Then she said, "Are you prepared to do this job the way it needs to be done?"

I nodded, but I could tell she wasn't convinced.

"If Mrs. Henry's going to pay you to clean her house," she continued, "that means you're taking on a responsibility. You will have to do what it takes to fulfill that responsibility. You need to be ready to do what it takes to make her happy she decided to hire you. You need to do what she says. You need to clean her house exactly the way she wants it cleaned—to do this job the right way and make that house shine. This is not a game, and it is not just a quick way for you to pick up some cash. This is a *commitment* you're making to Mrs. Henry. You are promising her you will make that house look just the way she wants it to look, to leave it better than you found it. Are you ready to make that commitment?"

I could tell from the expression on her face that she was not playing. This was serious. I was entering the world grown-ups lived in, the world my *mom* lived in, and it was a little scary. For a moment, I didn't speak.

She said, "Well?"

I responded, "Yes." And believe me, I meant it. I knew better than to try to put one over on my mom.

She nodded and said, "All right then. Tell her I said yes."

I called Mrs. Henry right away and told her the news.

That Saturday, I knocked on the door of Mrs. Henry's house, and she welcomed me in. She told me everything she wanted done, gave me the broom and the cleaning supplies I would need, asked me if I had any questions (I didn't), and said, "Let me know when you've finished, and I'll take a look at your work."

I took a deep breath, took hold of the broom, and started sweeping.

An hour later, having swept, dusted, polished, and scrubbed at what I thought was a major-league level, I went into the kitchen, found Mrs. Henry, and told her I was done.

"Let's see," she said. She led me into the living room, took one look, shook her head solemnly, and said "Oh no, dear. You're not done yet."

I reminded myself of my promise to my mom. I had told her I would listen to Mrs. Henry. Now, I knew, it was time to listen.

It was at this point that Mrs. Henry led me around the house and gave me a thorough master class in housecleaning. Her baseboards needed to be scrubbed in every possible crevice. Her pictures needed to be removed from the wall, dusted in all dimensions, and replaced. Her kitchen floor needed to be cleaned, by hand, with a damp, soapy rag, so that every last tiny stain her keen eye could detect was eliminated.

From my piano lessons, I already knew that Mrs. Henry was a stern, serious woman, someone you did not want to mess with. She could be very intimidating. That day, though, I sensed an underlying note of patience in her terse, no-nonsense assessment of my work so far. I could tell from that note of patience that everything would be all right between us if I just made sure to listen to her, do as she said, and never, ever try to cut corners.

After five or ten minutes of in-depth on-the-job training, she left me to my own devices once again.

For another hour, maybe a bit longer, I scrubbed, wiped, cleaned, swept, and dusted my heart out with full focus and intensity, reviewing every nook and cranny I had missed the first time and mindful of my promise to my mother and my commitment to Mrs. Henry. Looking back, I realize this was a pretty serious effort for a 12-year-old. At the time, though, all I was thinking of was that I wanted to make these two women proud of me. To do that, I knew I had to make that house shine, just as I had promised both of them I would.

I surveyed my work, decided I was ready, and went looking for Mrs. Henry.

We walked around the house together. She surveyed the work I had done and said nothing for the longest time. Then I saw a little smile break through on her face. She gave me five one-dollar bills (it seemed like a fortune to me!), and then she asked me to come back next week and do it all again. That night, when I showed my mom those five one-dollar bills and told her that Mrs. Henry wanted me to return, she smiled too.

Both of those smiles are etched in my memory.

That was a breakthrough day for me: I had a job, and I had earned that job. I had met Mrs. Henry's high standards. I had left that house better than I had found it. More importantly, I had left a *relationship* better than I had found it. And last but not least, I had met my mom's expectations.

When I was growing up, my mom often said to me, "Leave people and places better than you found them." Today, that's my calling. That's what I've been doing, in one form or another, since that day I first cleaned house for Mrs. Henry—even though I didn't refer to it as a calling back then. That's what I've committed myself to getting better at, time after time after time: leaving people and relationships better than I found them. And by the way, those words of my mother's, "Leave people and places better than you found them," eventually showed up on the wall of my company's corporate headquarters in Chicago. I tell you this, not to boast, but to illustrate the immense power of finding and pursuing your calling. I call the act of leveraging this power the Lighthouse Factor.

> Once you know your calling and commit yourself to pursuing it, that calling becomes clearer and clearer to you over time. You get better at recognizing when you are moving closer to it and when you are moving further away. Your calling is like a lighthouse beacon that gets brighter and larger on the horizon as you move toward it. You may not always have the perfect words for describing that light, but you always know when you're moving closer to it.

I've shared my experience with Mrs. Henry with you for a reason. I want you to find some similar incidents in your past and put the Lighthouse Factor to work in your own life.

DO THIS

Think back right now and identify at least one moment that serves as a beacon from your personal Lighthouse. This should be a moment that spotlights for you a time when you were certain—not just intrigued but certain—that you were headed in the right direction in your life. This could have happened when you were 12 years old or even younger. It could have happened yesterday. I don't know when it happened for you. But I know you can find a moment, or two, or three that illuminates your calling. All it takes is the willingness to pause, find some quiet time, and do a bit of self-exploration.

Take a few moments right now, before you continue reading any further, and think of a time when you knew you were doing the right thing, making the right contribution, and building the right skill set for the person you were meant to be. Notice that the action, the contribution, and the skill set should point in a *direction* that makes sense to you at a deep and enduring level—and that while the action, the contribution, and the skill set will change over time, the direction of your calling will not.

After you have devoted 30 to 60 minutes to the task of identifying one, two, or three such incidents, boil your calling down to a single sentence. This is your calling! Mine is *Leave things better than you found them.* What's yours? Write it down now. Then, once you have it, email it to me at (dee@couragebydesign.com) —and join the Courage Community!

18. YOUR CALLING AND YOUR PASSION ARE TWO DIFFERENT THINGS

"When a man truly commits, the universe will conspire to assure his success."

— *Henry David Thoreau*

Many people confuse their calling, their guiding purpose in life, with their passion. These are two very different things.

Your calling is the Lighthouse, that shining light beckoning you from the shore on the horizon. Your passion is the *fuel* you use to move closer toward that beacon. A passion is something you can give your all to, in service of your calling. Not every interest becomes a passion. Not every interest *stays* a passion.

Let me give you a couple of examples of what I mean. When I was 12 years old, cleaning a house was definitely something I felt total engagement about. This was my first job! So I was totally passionate about it and completely energized by the possibility of improving my relationship with Mrs. Henry—and making my mom proud, because I saw how hard she worked. Cleaning the house was getting me closer to the Lighthouse! It was something I could give my all to! But you know what? Time passes! Decades after I began cleaning Mrs. Henry's house, I am no longer scrubbing baseboards—but I am leaving people, situations, and relationships better than I found them. These days, somebody else cleans the house for me! And that's okay. As I say, not every interest stays a passion.

Here's another example. Shortly after I left the ad agency, I thought my destiny might be to become a chef. That matched up with my calling, I thought, because cooking for others had brought my mother a sense of deep fulfillment—and it certainly improved relationships and situations! Why couldn't becoming a chef do the same for me?

At that time, Charlie Trotter, a chef whose brilliance in the kitchen was internationally renowned, ran his eponymous Chicago restaurant in the Lincoln Park neighborhood. It was one of my favorite restaurants. Charlie opened it in 1987, and during its 25-year tenure, it won numerous awards and was widely considered to be one of the nation's best restaurants. While Charlie Trotter the chef had a massive impact on the world of cooking through his Michelin-starred restaurant, Charlie Trotter the teacher trained and mentored hundreds of aspiring cooks. I was one of them. I was fortunate enough to win a "guest chef" night at his restaurant! As the appointed evening drew near, my excitement grew. I could not wait to learn everything I could from Charlie.

It took just one day to open my eyes to the realities of a career in the culinary arts. By the end of that night, I was not passionate. I was exhausted—completely worn out. Sure, I had learned about being a sous chef, how kitchen mechanics work, and how to take orders and carry them out efficiently. But I had also learned that being on your feet for eight-plus hours, incessantly chopping and mixing, sautéing and searing, all the while monitoring and dodging and circling around the other members of the kitchen staff as they carried out their own food prep, was enormously demanding. I knew it was not for me. I knew it was not what I wanted to do for 10, 12, or even 14 hours a day.

I opted to transfer the love for food and cooking that I inherited from my mother into the role of restaurateur. *That,* it turned out, was something I had enduring passion for—and continue to have passion for, in my role helming Robinson Hill, an airport and travel venue concessionaire. I owe a debt of gratitude to Charlie Trotter; he opened my eyes to what my career should be and what direction I needed to take. And he helped me to get clarity on what I was truly passionate enough to spend most of my day doing—namely, running my own company! That way, I could leave customers and clients better than I had found them. I could leave employees better than I had found them. I could leave the community better than I had found it.

So I started looking at business ideas. That was, I discovered, something to which I could devote all my attention and energy for decades to come. (By the way, cooking and entertaining continue to be important parts of my life...but as a home chef.)

Take a closer look at what you wrote down and ask yourself: *Is this my calling in life...or is it a passion that I may not be as interested in a decade from now as I am today? Is this something to which I could see myself committing time and energy day after day for the foreseeable future?*

If what you wrote down is not your calling, revise it until it is! Once you have a concise statement of your calling in life, you can use it to keep yourself on track and to share with others who may be able to help you get closer to the Lighthouse.

Follow your calling and the universe will support you! When we commit to pursuing our calling, no matter what, extraordinary forces come to our aid...provided that we are willing and able to take action to make a place for those forces.

After I left that ad agency, after I figured out that being a chef was not the right path for me, I started a couple of business ventures. One failed quickly. The second showed promise, but it became clear to me soon enough that getting it off the ground would take more time, effort, creativity, and cash than I had anticipated. One morning, I looked at my bank account and realized I didn't have enough money to pay my rent. For a moment, I faltered. Was I really meant to be an entrepreneur? Or was I better off walking away from all this and getting a day job?

A voice inside me said, *You will find a way.*

I remember falling to my knees and praying for guidance toward that way. I didn't know what to do. I thought I had pursued every possible avenue. So I asked God for help. If I was meant to follow this path, would He help me to take the action I needed to take to keep moving forward on it?

And the moment I made that request, the name of a friend of mine flashed through my mind.

It was a long shot, but I decided to call him, explain my situation, and ask him to make a personal loan that would buy me enough time to get my business off the ground. I thought to myself, *This might work, or it might not—but I have to try.* I knew I wouldn't be able to say to myself that I had exhausted every opportunity until I picked up the phone, dialed the number, and made my case.

It wasn't easy. It was scary. But I did it.

And he agreed to loan me the money.

I took out the loan. I paid my rent. I kept my company. And I made a promise to myself that I would never, ever find myself in that situation again. That's a promise I've been able to keep. And yes, I repaid the loan in full. All thanks to the Lighthouse Factor.

We each have our own Lighthouse we're moving toward. Only you can spot yours. But once you do, you will know—because you will feel yourself getting more excited every time you do something that gets you closer to it!

One of my all-time favorite examples of a woman who knows the direction of her Lighthouse is business and finance legend Kay Koplovitz. Listen to her:

"HOW BIG CAN THIS GROW?"

In my experience, women are fearless in philanthropy, but they are not fearless when it comes to investing. For some reason, that's different to them. And that's what I'm out to change. We've got to be more fearless on the investment side, and we've got to do that by learning more about it. I've invested over many years, and I've had great returns and I've had failures. That's one of the things about investing. You've got to expect that not every investment turns out to be a home run. But failures shouldn't keep you from investing. You learn as you go; you make better decisions as you move forward. And I think that for a lot of women, maybe they didn't really have the investing responsibility in their family, or they relied on somebody else, whether it was their parents or their husband or their partner, or maybe an advisor, but for whatever reason they came to think, "Well, I really don't want to do this myself; it's too risky." And it's been a learning process, but that way of thinking is finally receding. There's a big difference between 20 years ago and today, because the women coming through today have had the opportunity to be exposed to the market.

Entrepreneurs understand the responsibility of taking in outside capital, and they are not afraid to do that today, whereas they were quite reticent to do it back in 2000, when I began this journey to support women founders raising capital. We have seen big changes in their preparedness to raise and deploy capital, elevating their vision for building a company to large scale and sustainability.

And I think that while we have made a big change in terms of expectations of where women can go, we still need to push the envelope on some questions that all good investors can learn to ask themselves: *How big can this grow? Where can we go from here? And how do we get there?*

We still need many, many more women on the investing side. I really feel it's important that women have the opportunity to invest in pre-IPO companies, which most women do not get the chance to do unless there is a vehicle, like Athena, for them to do it that is really open to inviting them in. There are a lot of changes happening in the marketplace, but I believe we still need more women to change their thinking. We need to see more women taking some of those dollars that in years past they might have had assigned to philanthropy and saying, "Look, what if I took 5 or 10 percent of those dollars I'm currently pointing toward philanthropy that I believe in and I invested them in a business that I believe in?"

I think that proposition is starting to take hold. Women

are finally starting to understand how and why they should get involved in investing. But we need more of them.

—**Kay Koplovitz, founder of USA Network,** of which she served as chairman & CEO from its founding in 1977 until 1998, when it was sold for $4.5 billion. Kay is the first woman ever to head a television network; she is currently (like me) a board member at Athena Consumer Acquisition Corp., SPAC.

For Kay, empowering women investors to succeed is what gets her closer to *her* Lighthouse. For me, being an entrepreneur is how I move closer to *my* Lighthouse. It's how I leave people better than I found them. It is the fullest expression of my calling.

How do you move closer to *your* Lighthouse?

19. BEFORE YOU MOVE ON TO THE SIXTH COMMANDMENT, DO THIS

QUESTIONS: COMMANDMENT V

- Have you ever sensed that there was something bigger in store for you? If so, what is it? (Take plenty of time in composing a written answer to this question.)

- What is your "big why"—your calling in life? What did your Higher Power put you on earth to do? What is the Lighthouse you are moving toward? (Take plenty of time in composing a written answer to this question.)

- Who is—or could be—your "calling ally"? Make a list of 5–10 people. Then assess the list and find 2 or 3 who provide the best fit. If you like, you can make one of them me by subscribing to the monthly COURAGE BY DESIGN e-newsletter. Email me at dee@couragebydesign.com.

- Are you still taking personal private time—time just to be quiet, all by yourself—each day? If not, please re-engage with this commitment before you move on to the next commandment. This is how you build up the Courage to Hear, the Courage to Dream Big, and the Courage to Do the Right Thing.

ACTIONS: COMMANDMENT V

- Review your answers to the questions above and use them to create a one-sentence summary of your personal calling in life. (As an example, mine is *to leave people and places better than I found them.*)

- Show the summary *only* to people you trust to encourage you and support you. Ask them whether they think that what you have written about what you aim to be, do, contribute, and become reflects the best possible version of you.

Once you have done all this, you will be ready to move on to Commandment VI.

COMMANDMENT VI

Leverage Your Strong Suit

MAXIMIZE

"Do more of what you love,
less of what you tolerate,
and none of what you hate."

—John Assaraf

20. SPOT THE ARROW

> "Don't push your weaknesses.
> Play to your strengths."
>
> —Jennifer Lopez

Years ago, I noticed an arrow hurtling through the air and learned to follow it. If I hadn't learned to follow that arrow, you wouldn't be reading these words.

When I didn't have enough money to pay my rent, something within me sent a familiar message: *You can't do this.* When I heard that message, I considered walking away from entrepreneurship and finding another job. But before that notion could take hold and grow roots in my mind, I did what I've been training you to do: I told the irrational fear that I had no time for it. I refused to let myself go down that path. I decided it was time for me to banish the inner critic who insisted on lobbing snide comments—like "You can't do this"—my way.

The self-pity and fear that the inner critic was trying to sell me were pointing me down a familiar path, but I saw in that moment that self-pity and fear were not serving me. I knew I needed to replace my limiting beliefs and my unproductive internal dialogue with one rooted in courage and power. I did what I have been training you to do. I reframed and moved forward. I told myself, *I'm good at this.*

It was difficult to prepare myself to talk to someone about borrowing money. But once I *did* pick up the phone and dial, it got easier. And once I started the conversation, it got easier still. It was at that point that I noticed something interesting: I actually *was* good at this!

I was in the groove. I was talking about possibilities. I was talking about initiatives that I knew with certainty would impact other people, and me, in a powerful, positive, measurable way. I was enrolling someone else in an exciting idea.

And it worked. Who knew?

That feeling of being in the groove was the arrow. The fateful conversation with my friend, I realized, had simply been a matter of following that arrow. The arrow hurtling through the air was *me, leveraging my strong suit.* I followed mine. You can follow yours.

In a matter of seconds, I knew that this kind of conversation felt very different from me trying to be a chef. It felt *energizing*—far more energizing than anything I had done at the ad agency. Why? Because it was about *my* future and *my* business! It was about possibilities that *I* had designed and the value *I* wanted to deliver! I loved talking to people about those things!

I started looking for other ways I could leverage my strong suit.

I knew that if my business were to survive and thrive, I'd need to scale up significantly—and quickly. I knew my product—high-end corporate gift baskets—was good, but I also knew I needed to find a way to grow large enough to be able to buy my materials in bulk. To achieve this, I needed a corporate partner. I'd done my research, and I was determined to get into Sears. So I decided to leverage my strong suit again.

I resolved to call Sears's VP of Licensed Business, a gentleman named Lou. One way or another, I would enroll Lou in the idea of buying gift baskets from my company.

Days, then weeks went by. I tried relentlessly to get through to Lou. The gatekeepers always seemed to be in my way. Oddly, I found this motivating—it was like a puzzle I was supposed to solve. I got curious about the obstacle and how I could overcome it! Finally, I had the bright idea to call Lou's number after 7:00 P.M., when it seemed likely that the gatekeepers would have left for the day. One evening, he answered the phone.

I could tell from his tone he was thinking, *Oh boy, I got caught.* I quickly pitched him my corporate gift basket idea, describing how well-crafted and intricate and thoughtful they were. Lou told me that Sears did indeed buy gift baskets but that they already had an exclusive contract with an outside vendor.

I was crushed, but I still had that strong suit that I knew I could leverage: enrolling people in possibilities. I could still follow that arrow!

Now that I had gotten Lou on the phone, after all that effort and planning and all those calls, what was I going to do—hang up? Of course not! If Lou didn't want to talk about plan A, I would share some ideas about plan B. In fact, being ready to talk about plan B had been part of my "battle plan" for engaging with Lou all along!

I had done my due diligence, and I knew that Sears wanted to reach beyond its core suburban customer base and attract a growing, ethnically diverse urban clientele. I also knew that Sears wanted to return to its downtown Chicago Loop location someday down the road, and to do that, its retail offerings in that location would need to reflect the diversity of the surrounding area. I also knew that there was a burgeoning interest at the time in Afrocentric merchandise (this was 1993). I had faith that this was no mere fad, as indeed it was not.

Switching gears, I pitched Lou my plan B: a small in-store boutique, Unity Square, that would sell African-inspired and authentic merchandise that could attract the diverse clientele Sears was targeting. I described the products I wanted to carry and assured Lou that I would handle all the details necessary to have the boutique in place in time for holiday purchasing. Guess what happened? Lou started leaning into my message, rather than leaning away from it. Because I had done my due diligence, because I was offering value, and because I was leveraging my strong suit, this was an easy proposition to lean into. There would be little to no risk to Sears in the Unity Square initiative. I would run it as a licensed business.

We talked for what must have been half an hour, but it felt to me like only a couple of minutes. Lou asked to see a formal business plan. When I got off that initial call with Lou, I felt like I could walk on air.

This, I knew, was *definitely* something I was good at doing. That focused conversation, a conversation I had launched and driven, had gotten me where I needed to go, it had gotten Lou where he needed to go, and it had opened up doors to massive new opportunities. Planning, initiating, and sustaining that kind of conversation, I realized, was my groove. Unlike prepping and overseeing a five-star restaurant's kitchen for a full night of cooking, this was definitely something I could do for years or decades into the future. This was the arrow that pointed toward *me at my very best.*

You've heard of call avoidance, the phenomenon under which people don't want to make phone calls where they might get rejected? I had the exact opposite. I was primed to make phone calls to as many people as I needed! If they opted not to work with me, that would be their loss. I could come up with a plan A, a plan B, and even a plan C for any number of allies who hadn't yet heard of me or my business. And I could feel totally fulfilled doing that!

Long story short—I ended up closing that deal with Sears, and as a result, I was on my way as an entrepreneur. Why? Because I had isolated—and developed—one of my strong suits: *enrolling other people in ideas of mutual benefit.*

Each of us has one or more personal strong suits. This is a special kind of expertise—an area where we consistently add value to the experience and outcomes of other people *and* at the same time derive deep joy from doing so.

> Your strong suit is you at your best. It's something you do that consistently adds value to the experiences and outcomes of other people…*and* at the same time gives you deep personal joy.

Notice that I used the word *and*. A strong suit must fulfill both of these criteria.

If you add value but do not experience joy as you do that, you're not yet looking at your strong suit. By the same token, if you're experiencing joy but you're not delivering value, not making it easier for anyone else to accomplish something that's important to them, *that's* not your strong suit, either. Keep looking until you spot the arrow. This search takes courage—sometimes a great deal of courage. And so does the decision to focus on your strong suit when others are expecting you to do something else!

21. STRONG SUIT OR CALLING?

> ## "What makes you different or weird—
> ## that's your strength."
> — *Meryl Streep*

Your strong suit is different from your calling. This is an extremely important point!

Your calling is what you were put on earth to do. Your strong suit is the specific action or actions you take *in support of* your calling that deliver(s) measurable value to others.

> Your calling is what you were put on earth to do. Your strong suit is the specific action or actions you take *in support of* your calling that deliver(s) measurable value to others.

You have one calling in life. You may have many, many strong suits—or you may have just one. You cannot fulfill your calling without leveraging your strong suit.

For example: My calling is leaving people, situations, and relationships better than I found them. One of the strong suits I deploy in support of that calling is *enrolling someone else in ideas that excite and inspire both of us to take action and make things better.*

I'm good at that. My ability to do it adds value to the experiences and outcomes of others. And doing it gives me deep personal joy. It's one of my strong suits. That's not boasting, by the way. It's self-awareness.

Another strong suit I've got is *picking talented people and helping them grow and contribute.* I enjoy hiring the right person for the right job, hiring people who are smarter than I am, supporting those people and giving them exactly what they need to succeed and contribute. I *love* doing all that. That strong suit has led to substantial growth for my company.

Whenever I ask myself, *Is this the best use of my time?* I know that if I am leveraging either of these strong suits at the level I am capable of, the answer is going to be *yes*! And if the answer is *no*, I know I am looking, not at a strong suit, but at a potential area of weakness. It is important to know the difference between a strong suit and a weakness…and to build up the courage necessary to step away from weaknesses so you can play to your strengths. (By the way, I've written the words "Is this the best use of my time?" on a sticky note and posted that note near my computer screen so I can see it multiple times during the workday!)

DO THIS

Ask yourself: "Is this the best use of my time?" Jot down that sentence on a sticky note and post it somewhere you will see it throughout the day.

I know what my strong suits are, and you should, too. Learn to recognize when you are investing time, effort, and energy in your strong suits and when you are not. Look for opportunities to lean into your strong suits.

Let me be clear about something important here: When Lou tried to get me off the phone, it took courage for me to plant my feet and redirect the conversation to plan B. It would have been easy—and comfortable—for me to walk down the path of "You have a nice day; let's keep in touch." It would have been easy for me to waste time and energy feeling crushed and full of regret the moment he tried to brush me off.

But it would not have been leveraging my strong suit, and it would not have been fair to me, to Lou, or to Sears.

> Noticing and prioritizing your strong suit often means challenging the status quo—and summoning the courage necessary to move past that status quo.

Is it always easy to move beyond your comfort zone and learn to leverage your strong suit? No. Does it take a little practice to challenge someone else's expectations, as I challenged Lou's? Of course. But what is the alternative? *Doing what you have always done will generate the results you have always generated.* Find what you do best—and find a way to do more of that!

By the way, even if you feel you already have a good sense of what your strong suit is, I want to encourage you to engage fully in everything you're about to encounter. My job here is to help you build up the courage to move away from the familiar—and identify some strong suits you didn't even know you had!

22. IN THE FLOW

> "Master your strengths,
> outsource your weaknesses."
> — *Ryan Khan*

When I ask people I'm coaching if they know what their strong suit is, I find that they typically have one of two immediate responses. The first group more or less instantly gets what I'm talking about. People in this group say things like, "My strong suit is turning the spoken word into the written word in a powerful way. I could do that all day. Sometimes I can't believe people actually pay me to do it." Or: "My strong suit is taking graphics and visual design to the next level for people who want to make a major impact in their marketing collateral and product design. That's what people pay me to do, and I love doing it." There are an infinite number of possible strong suits, of course, so people can fill in these blanks in any number of impossible-to-predict ways. But the point is, *they know exactly what I mean.*

The people in the second group, though, have a very different response. It's almost as though they didn't hear my definition of a strong suit. They look at me in a kind of puzzled way and say things like, "I guess I'd have to say that I'm pretty good at numbers. I work spreadsheets very efficiently." And I'll ask, "Do you *love* working with numbers? Do you find yourself wanting to do it even when you aren't getting paid for it?" And they'll say, "Well, no."

Or by the same token, I'll get people in that second group who will say something like, "I love baseball. I could talk baseball all day long." Then I'll ask: "Is there any part of your loving baseball that delivers value—value that other people are willing to pay for?" And they'll say, "Well, no."

If you find yourself in that second group—if you feel like you're coming up empty when you're asked what your strong suit is—don't worry. You're just one good coaching conversation away from putting yourself into that first group, where you belong. Having that kind of conversation is what I want you and me to experience right now. Courage means identifying your strong suit and playing to it! Fear means sticking with the status quo!

When you're leveraging your strong suit, the line between work and play blurs and vanishes. Learning to notice when that happens and finding a way to make sure it happens as often as possible are important parts of living a courageous life.

There is a name that psychologists give to the experience I call "leveraging your strong suit." They call it "flow" or "motivational flow," and the way they describe this state gives us important clues about how to spot the activity and the skill set we're talking about. They point out that this experience is enjoyable—as distinct from pleasurable. There's a difference. Take a look at this explanation from *PositivePsychology.com*:

"Flow experiences are active, while pleasurable experiences are typically passive and fleeting. Flow is neither good nor bad. It simply is. Flow can lead to experiencing life more fully and intensely. We can experience more meaning. It also can strengthen how we define who we are."[9]

When you find yourself losing yourself in something you know is pointing you in the right direction and you don't need any motivation from the outside in order to do it, *that's leveraging your strong suit.*

If what you are doing leaves you feeling more fulfilled, more grateful, more energized, more alive, *that's leveraging your strong suit.*

When you look back at the value you've delivered while you are "in the flow," and you think, *That's who I am; that's what I am supposed to be doing with my life*, that's leveraging your strong suit. (For me, it feels like conducting a symphony. I don't know what it feels like to you, but I do know you have to find out.)

Whenever you experience the kind of moment I'm talking about, a moment of being in the flow, *notice it!* Write something down about it! Talk about it! Then find a way to focus more of your time, energy, and attention on it!

Set aside, for the moment, the expectations of other people. Set aside the status quo. Focus like a laser beam on taking action on what you enjoy and can get lost in. Set aside time on the calendar when you don't have to think about bosses, or parents, or teachers, or peers, or anyone else who doesn't happen to benefit *directly* from what you have to offer when you are leveraging your strong suit. Experience the enjoyment you get from actively contributing something of value to someone else's world. That enjoyment is the arrow that will point you toward a strong suit you can leverage in support of your calling.

Knowing your strong suit is what makes miracles possible. I'll tell you how I know that: personal experience.

Within only a matter of days, my first business idea—the gift basket concept—had officially failed, swiftly and decisively. But I was still standing; my company was still intact, I had a major corporate partnership, and I was more determined than ever to move forward from it and deliver success for my partners, my stakeholders, my customers, and myself. I was on the cusp of launching a new business, with an innovative concept, and I was excited. Unity Square, my first successful business, was born. It thrived for almost a decade—all because I learned to recognize the arrow that was pointing me toward my strong suits.

"THAT'S WHAT I DO"

I always thought that one of the stupidest things that people can ask job applicants during interviews is, "Where do you personally want to be five years from now?" You know what my standard answer was to that question? I would say, "I don't know, but I do know that I'll be working with smart and fun people, and I know that I'll be learning every day. I know I'll be finding the right people to help me on the things that I can't do myself, and I know I'll be embracing new opportunities. That's kind of what I do." That was my honest answer, and I think it's a good answer.

Particularly when you are a leader of others, I believe surrounding yourself with people who are smarter than you are in what they need to do is one of the most important things you can do, because you can't do everything. I never trust people who say they can do everything or act as if they can do everything because I just know it's not true. I'm not good at everything. I don't pretend I know more about finance than the finance person or that I know more about operations than the COO. I am good at surrounding myself with people who are smarter than I am, pointing them toward a goal and a vision that we can all agree on as important, having good discussions, listening to them, and making decisions. That's what I do.

I see a lot of CEOs who are not really interested in having discussions with their leadership teams. Basically, they just want an execution team; they say, "We're going to go do A, B, C, and D; go make that happen," and then the execution team goes and does it. That's not how I view leadership at all. I think you get the best ideas and the best solutions from the team from letting everybody contribute. And yeah, in the end, somebody needs to make the final decision, and based on all the information you have, that is probably you. But if you don't listen, if you don't have input from as many diverse sources as possible, they're not going to be the best decisions.

—**Karen van Bergen,**
executive vice president, dean, Omnicom University;
chief environmental sustainability officer at Omnicom

Karen is a textbook example of someone who knows exactly what her strong suit is and how to lean into it. (Sidenote: She is absolutely right. I can attest, from personal experience, to the importance of empowering people and then getting out of their way.)

Follow Karen's lead! Identify and leverage your strong suit.

DO THIS

Identify and leverage your strong suit.

It's time to spot *your* arrow. Take the time you need to identify one specific activity that you are *not* spending a lot of time on but that matches up with *all* of the following criteria:

➡ You feel engaged and empowered when you do this.

➡ You inspire and engage others when you do this.

➡ You and others are proud of the outcomes you deliver when you do this.

➡ You are willing to conduct due diligence before you do this so as to deliver value for a specific person, organization, or group.

➡ You create new possibilities and new opportunities for yourself and others when you do this.

➡ Others you trust say you are good at this.

➡ You know, deep down, that this is the best use of your time.

Your strong suits may not be ones you have read about here. I am not saying you need to identify *my* strong suits. I am challenging you to identify *yours*. (Note: The questions you answered in chapter 15 may help you identify your strong suits and the activities that connect to them.)

Once you have isolated an activity that leverages a strong suit to which you are not fully committed, I want you to set an appointment with yourself. Find at least 15 minutes a day to *execute* on that strong suit...keep that appointment...and make that strong suit part of your personal identity! It is who you truly are. Claim it!

23. BEFORE YOU MOVE ON TO THE SEVENTH COMMANDMENT, DO THIS

QUESTIONS: COMMANDMENT VI

- Did you complete the DO THIS activity at the end of chapter 22? If not now, then when?

- What is one of your strong suits? If you're struggling to answer this, what have you been repeatedly told by others that you do well? Others can often see your gifts before you acknowledge them. Describe your gift briefly.

- What value does it deliver to others?

- When was the last time you executed it?

- When or how will you execute it next? With whom?

- Are you still taking personal private time—time just to be quiet, all by yourself—each day? If not, please re-engage with this commitment before you move on to the next commandment.

ACTIONS: COMMANDMENT VI

- Expand the amount of time you spend leveraging the strong suit you just identified. Summon the courage necessary to move past the status quo. Claim and take action on who you truly are, not by pushing your weaknesses, but by playing to your strengths.

- When leveraging your strong suit, be prepared to challenge the expectations of others in a way that serves everyone.

Once you have done all this, you will be ready to move on to Commandment VII.

COMMANDMENT VII

Connect with Allies Who Are Focused on Solutions

CONNECT

"When people tell you
who they are, believe them."

— Maya Angelou

24. JOIN THE CLUB

"Do not be concerned with the fruit of your action—just give attention to the action itself. The fruit will come of its own accord. This is a powerful spiritual practice."

— *Eckhart Tolle*

We each face Moments of Truth when it comes to following this seventh commandment. Let me tell you about one of mine. Just a few weeks into my first year as an undergraduate at Penn, I came face to face with the problem of invisibility.

As an African American woman, I quickly learned that there were people on campus who would not allow me on their radar screen—people who would not even say "hello" to me. For them, I did not exist. I could walk past them and look at them and smile, and they would keep their eyes straight ahead or look down and tune me out. Sometimes, just to make a point, I would say "HELLO!" in a voice that was loud and purposeful enough that it couldn't possibly be ignored. There are times when you've got to grab that control and let people know that they cannot dismiss you.

At Penn, there was a place called DuBois House—a special residence set aside for primarily African American students on campus. I understood the need for such a place and was glad it was there. I wanted to experience everything Penn had to offer. I wanted my money's worth. I wanted to give the best I could possibly give. I wanted to be challenged and take chances, and I wanted to see what I was truly capable of. In the process, I wanted to connect with as many different kinds of people and different ways of thinking as I could.[*]

But I had a challenge. I was uncomfortable speaking up in public. I knew this was something I needed to work on. Public speaking certainly isn't the obstacle it once was for me, but in my freshman year, it *was* still an obstacle for me.

One evening, a friend of mine and I went to a meeting of the Student Activity Council (SAC). My friend was encouraging me to stand up during this meeting and put myself forward as a candidate for a position in student government. He also thought I would make a good chair of the Finance Committee. First, I needed to get elected to the SAC. Even though I knew I would do the job well, getting it meant standing up and making my case during this meeting. That felt a little too close to speaking in front of an audience.

I sat there for an hour or so and listened to all the speakers making their cases for election to the SAC. At one point, I heard a voice say, "Is there anyone else?" There were knots in my stomach, but I could also

---

[*] As a sidenote, let me make the point that affinity groups like those that gather at DuBois House are essential. We need them, and we will always need them. The world would be a far worse place without them. They are safe circles where people can listen to each other and be there for each other. At the same time, we need to know that those of us who love places like DuBois house, who use them, who support them and keep them going, will eventually face a critical question: How and when do we move beyond them? How do we take the problems that we've defined and shared in that all-important safe circle into a setting where we can *solve* the problems? This is a journey each of us must make, the journey from solace to solution that is discussed in depth in the next chapter. While we are on the subject of safe circles, I cannot talk about Penn without mentioning the legendary Harold Haskins. He wanted resources for every minority student who ever appeared on Penn's campus, and he made sure they had the support and tools they needed to succeed. He recognized the uneven playing field and worked passionately to close the gap.

feel the regret that would haunt me if I didn't stand up for something I wanted.

I will be honest with you. I was daunted by the prospect of standing up and saying even a single word in front of that group. Would I embarrass myself? Would I lose? I froze in fear at the thought of attempting to tell any of them why I was the best person for the role. But I could also feel the importance of the moment that had presented itself to me, and I knew that moment was slipping away.

This was my Moment of Truth. Something deep inside told me to stand up and start talking. I had no idea what I was about to say, but I stood up and said it anyway. I already knew why: I could make a difference. I could leave Penn better than I had found it. So I spoke from my heart about my commitment and my contribution.

I wish I'd had a tape recorder going when I started speaking, because in retrospect it was obvious that this was one of the most important events of my life. I'd love to be able to share with you verbatim what I shared with that group, but I can't, so I will just tell you from memory that what came out of my mouth unbidden was what I felt most strongly about during my first few weeks at Penn: that there were some students who weren't getting all they could out of the university experience, who weren't exposing themselves to new ideas, new people, and new resources. That there were students who were marking time here when they could be getting more from an institution as amazing as our school. That I wasn't going to miss out on what Penn had to offer. That I wanted to stretch myself and see what I was capable of learning and doing. That I wanted others to be empowered to do the same. And that if I was elected to the SAC as chair of the Finance Committee, I would do my level best to make sure the people who could benefit from the resources entrusted to me got the chance to use them, benefit from them, and find out what they were truly capable of at our school.

When I sat back down, my friend gave me a hug. And a few moments after that, I won the election. Experiences like this give us momentum, but we still have to call on our courage over and over again.

Now, here's the moral of the story: By listening to my friend, by stepping up, by claiming my power, by setting high standards, by expressing what I believed in and was willing to take a stand for, *I gained membership in a special club.* Today I call that club the Sailors on the Sea of Agency—the people who have taken a stand and who are taking action to solve a problem. Those kinds of people are drawn to each other.

> ## DO THIS
> Think of yourself as a Sailor on the Sea of Agency. Look for other sailors to connect with. Remember: agency means the capacity to act independently and set your own course.

And let me make it very clear: I'm not just talking about students at Penn. Almost immediately, I established important alliances with fellow travelers on the Sea of Agency who were serving as professors and members of Penn's Board of Trustees. I had working relationships with these people! Even though we had different roles to play and huge gaps in age and experience, *we were in the same club.* And some of those relationships, thank God, have endured from that day to this.

Don't miss the next Moment of Truth that comes your way. Capitalize on it by doing three simple things:

- Set a high personal standard for yourself—a high personal aspiration.

- Figure out what you are willing to take a stand for and whom you are serving.

- Find a problem that you are committed to solving on a personal level, and take action to make a solution happen.

If you do those three things, you won't have to worry about "networking." People will be drawn to you, just as they were drawn to me. You will find yourself sailing on the Sea of Agency, and along the way you will find like-minded individuals who want to be your ally.

DO THIS

➡ Set a high personal standard for yourself—a high personal aspiration.

➡ Figure out what you are willing to take a stand for and whom you are serving.

➡ Find a problem that you are committed to solving on a personal level, and take action to make a solution happen.

Other good things will start happening to you, too. I speak from experience on this point. I leaned into other opportunities and built more connections that became possible once I embraced and acted on my Moment of Truth.

After I won that election, I noticed that people who had once stared right past me started saying "hello" to me when I passed them in the halls on the way to class. I may have earned their respect, but sadly, instead of wanting to know me, some smiled only because I was now chair of the Finance Committee, overseeing the budgets of every student organization.

"BUT I'M AN INTROVERT!"

This seventh commandment, I find, intimidates people at first, particularly people who consider themselves introverts or "not good at networking." In order to get the most from this part of the book, you will want to set aside such beliefs about yourself, if you have them. Forget all about networking for a moment. Forget all about introverts and extroverts, too. Forget all about whether you consider yourself a "people person." None of this is relevant to fulfilling this commandment. If you think of alliance-building as serving others with the solutions you can provide, you will find it far easier to build alliances with the right people. The key is to focus on *action*.

My challenge to you with this commandment is a simple one: *get over whatever is holding you back from doing these three things:*

- setting a high personal standard for yourself—a high personal aspiration;
- figuring out what you are willing to take a stand for and whom you are serving; and

- finding a problem that you are committed to solving on a personal level and taking action to make a solution happen.

What is stopping these things from happening right now in your life? It might be a fear of speaking in public. It might be a dysfunctional belief that you are unqualified to share your opinions and experiences. It might be a myth you have bought into that you are not a "good networker." It might be a story you have been telling yourself for years about how you are not a "people person." It might be any of a hundred other excuses. None of those excuses matter now. Set them aside. Fixating on those (imagined) obstacles will only cause you to miss your next Moment of Truth.

Just ask yourself: What is your high personal aspiration? What are you out to make happen at the highest possible level of quality and attention? What standard are you prepared to hold yourself to? What are you willing to take a stand for? What will you never, ever compromise? Whom are you serving by taking this stand? What problem are you personally committed to solving?

Knowing and communicating the answers to these questions will draw the right people into your orbit. That's because the people who sail on the Sea of Agency instantly notice and recognize one another. They spot each other from far away and feel instantly comfortable in each other's company. People who sail on the Sea of Agency look for ways to support each other. And here's the best part: it is never a chore or a drain of energy for them to lend a hand to an ally who is making a journey on that same sea; it is always empowering.

25. FROM SOLACE TO SOLUTION

"Focus on the solution, not the problem."
—*Jim Rohn*

Rohn's advice is powerful and life-changing. It has been my die-hard standard since I shifted to an entrepreneurial, solution-focused, and abundance mindset. When faced with a problem, I immediately shift my thinking to, "How can I fix this? What value can I add?" Yours should, too.

Have you ever been in a meeting where most people were spending their time and attention talking about the problem with very little time pondering the solution? That's not the kind of meeting we want to be in! We know what the problem is. We need resolution! I specialize in 80/20 meetings: 80 percent of the time is focused on solutions and only 20 percent on problems. When entering my office to address a problem, members of my team must walk in the door with ideas on how to fix that problem.

One of the most important pieces of coaching I give people is to relentlessly search out the path that takes them from a *solace* mindset to a *solution* mindset. Finding this path always involves *building or reinforcing alliances with other people who are just as focused on solutions as we are*. This is a critical element of the seventh commandment.

Solace is what happens when we talk compassionately with other people about a problem that exists, and we mean what we say. Solace is someone we respect telling us, "I get what you're going through, and I'm sorry you're having to go through it." Solace, in other words, is the expression of human empathy. Don't misunderstand: There is nothing wrong with solace. Our lives would be empty without it.

Solace has its place. We could be giving or receiving solace about a logistical problem, such as a working process that needs to be fixed. We could be giving or receiving solace about a cultural problem, such as a pervasive attitude from a coworker that marginalizes certain people in the organization—an attitude that doesn't match up with the organization's stated values. We could be giving or receiving solace about a business problem, such as a technological advance that we think our organization hasn't yet built a strategy around, a pricing decision we feel is out of step with the market, or an initiative from a competitor that we feel senior leadership hasn't paid enough attention to. All of these workplace examples are potentially very serious challenges. When they impact us or people we like and respect, we are right to move into *solace* mode: connecting with others, empathizing with others, sharing our own feelings about what's happened, acknowledging that the problem exists, and supporting those who have to deal with it.

But we can't stop there.

We have to ask ourselves, *How do I move forward toward a solution to this problem? And with whom?*

> **DO THIS**
> Ask yourself: *How do I move forward toward a solution to this problem? And with whom?*

When I talk about moving from solace to solution, I am not by any stretch of the imagination asking you to eliminate solace from your life. I am not saying you should not be part of an affinity group that supports you and understands you. Solace is important. Solace matters. Solace has to happen. But if we stop there, we don't claim agency in our own world. And that's a huge mistake.

We have to start finding the path toward *solving* the problem we have uncovered…and that means building and strengthening certain special relationships. I'm talking about relationships that are based on three shared values that connect to what I shared with you in the previous chapter:

- having high standards and high aspirations (two sides of the same coin),
- knowing exactly what you stand for and whom you are serving, and
- being willing and able to take action to solve a problem whose solution matters to you personally.

If we stop at *solace,* we may never live these values consistently. We may get stuck at the level of the support group. On the other hand, if we keep going toward a solution, we become part of that special group of action-oriented leaders I call Sailors on the Sea of Agency.

These kinds of leaders do not limit themselves to relationships with people whose aspirations and standards are low, who are still figuring out what they stand for, and who are not yet conditioned to take effective action to solve a problem. In other words, they don't stop at *solace.* They understand the "support group" mindset, but they don't restrict themselves to discussions with people who are supportive, people who are perhaps facing the same kinds of problems they are facing, people who will empathize with their situation and expect them to empathize with theirs. They also want relationships with people who take action to change things.

There is nothing wrong with having a support group, of course. We may need to be part of a group like that. There are times when being part of a group like that—one that will allow us to heal, recalibrate, recharge, and help others to do the same—is exactly what we need. But if we never move *beyond* the support group, if we never take action to *solve* the problems we are talking about, we may just find ourselves swimming in a sea of despair. And that's not where we want to be.

It's when we move from *solace* to *solution* that we truly set sail on the Sea of Agency.

You will know someone who is supposed to be your ally because they, like you...

- have high standards and high aspirations (these are two sides of the same coin),

- know exactly what they stand for and whom they are serving, and

- are willing to take action to create a solution.

Invest some time into building a relationship with this person! This is who you want to be with...and who you want to be.

This is the person you want to get feedback from. This is the person whose example you want to study. This is a fellow Sailor on the Sea of Agency. You want to connect with as many of these people as possible. They will help you build up courage in critical areas of your life, and you will do the same for them.

26. YOUR ARMOR

"Despair shows us the limit of our imagination. Imagination shared creates collaboration, and collaboration creates community, and community inspires social change."

—Terry Tempest Williams

The seventh commandment is all about building relationships that focus on solutions.

I tell people I'm coaching, "If you want to bring about a solution, don't *just* talk to the people in your current circle. Don't *just* talk to the people who will listen to you when you talk about what isn't working. Expand your circle. Talk to people who can take action to solve the problem too.

Be an ally who focuses on solutions. This is the best way to attract allies who focus on solutions."

> Be an ally who focuses on solutions. This is the best way to attract allies who focus on solutions.

Very often, when we are in "support group" mode, we will find ourselves surrounded by people who are facing obstacles that are similar or identical to the problems we're facing, people who want solace and will give solace in return. Whether the problem we are facing is logistical, cultural, strategic, or something else entirely, it may be tempting to invest most or all of our social energy in such groups. Why? Because we're being supported! People are validating us! But there comes a point where we need to ask ourselves: *Am I learning anything new here? Am I growing, learning, and moving forward as a person? Am I any closer to a solution to the problem I'm facing? Am I sailing on the Sea of Agency or the Sea of Despair?* If we don't like the answers we hear to those questions, we need to search out some additional people to talk to.

Here's a strategy that has proven effective for me: find a way to bring into the discussion at least *two* critical decision-makers with the authority to influence change and make something positive happen.

> **DO THIS**
>
> Identify two people who can work with you to *take action* to solve whatever problem you've identified.

If there's only one person in your conversation who can influence the change you want, your options are limited; you're basically restrained by that relationship. But if you can find and engage *two* people who can make something positive happen, you have a lot more options when it comes to the creating solutions.

Following the seventh commandment—connecting with allies who are focused on solutions—is integral to the discipline that I call *solution-based leadership.* It's a style of working, of interacting, of attracting others to your cause. It is a style of *living* that focuses not just on problems, but on *relationships* that bring about solutions.

We too often forget what we are made of and who made us. The people I call Sailors on the Sea of Agency are there to remind us. With the right relationships to support us, we really can figure anything out, no matter how fearful we may be at any given moment. Sometimes, the relationship we need is with someone who can take action in tandem with us to create a solution. And sometimes, the relationship we need is with someone who will coach us and push us a little bit on how to create the solution ourselves. We need both kinds of allies. And the very best place to find them is on the Sea of Agency.

I can't tell you the number of times I turned to my mother for help finding answers to major problems I was facing. Sometimes she would work side by side with me to create the right solution to the challenge… but more often she would simply say, "You will figure it out." Honestly, this would frustrate me to no end. I wanted answers! Little did I know how well she was preparing me for the life I would be leading.

My mother was the ultimate Sailor on the Sea of Agency, and she never let herself drift onto the Sea of Despair. She had the wisdom to know when to offer guidance and collaboration…and when to challenge me to go out and find the answers on my own. The faith my mother had and helped me cultivate became impenetrable armor for me. It is the unwavering belief that I can *always* figure it out, either on my own or by creating a relationship with someone with agency who is willing to partner with me in identifying solutions and taking action. Donning this armor has enabled me to safely navigate countless dangerous roads so that I crossed into vast plains of discovery and empowerment. And it can do the same for you.

27. BEFORE YOU MOVE ON TO THE EIGHTH COMMANDMENT, DO THIS

QUESTIONS: COMMANDMENT VII

- Who is currently in your inner circle who might not belong there? Make a list. Who belongs in your inner circle and isn't yet there? Make a list.

- Right now, are you sailing on the Sea of Despair or the Sea of Agency? How do you know? Are you more interested in solace or solutions? On which do you spend most of your time during a typical day?

- Do you regularly propose solutions to important problems? Are you comfortable doing so in front of a group? When was the last time that happened?

- What standard will you never compromise? What do you stand for? What problem are you personally committed to solving?

- Are you still taking personal private time—time just to be quiet, all by yourself—each day? If not, please re-engage with this commitment before you move on to the next commandment. This is how you build up the Courage to Hear, the Courage to Dream Big, and the Courage to Do the Right Thing.

ACTIONS: COMMANDMENT VII

- Be prepared to discuss what you stand for, what problems you are personally committed to solving, and why it is important to solve them.
- In any situation you face today, think and speak more about adding value and focusing on solutions to shared problems.
- Be an ally who focuses on solutions. This is the best way to attract allies who focus on solutions.

Once you have done all this, you will be ready to move on to Commandment VIII.

COMMANDMENT VIII

Choose Whom You Do (and Don't) Share Your Dream With

BUILD THE CIRCLE

"Dreams do come true, but not without the help of others, a good education, a strong work ethic, and the courage to lean in."

—Ursula Burns

28. THE HUMAN ROADBLOCK

"Never make someone a priority when
all you are to them is an option."

— *Maya Angelou*

Recently, I was privileged to go on a powerful weekend retreat with 15 of the most accomplished, successful, and highly motivated women in the world.

I can't tell you their names because I promised not to compromise the confidentiality of the event. But believe me when I tell you that these were *all* women who had built up extraordinary levels of personal, financial, and charitable success in their lives—all of them, as the poet Arthur O'Shaughnessy put it, were true "movers and shakers."[10] Maybe the best way to describe them is simply to say I felt honored to be in that room, not just because of the accomplishments of the women around me, but because it was such a welcoming, loving space. We were all there for each other. Madeleine Albright once said, "There's a place in hell for women who don't help each other."[11] Well, this entire group will undoubtedly go to heaven.

The high point of the retreat came when we all spoke up and shared our major goals for the coming years. The idea was that by speaking our goals out loud and by supporting each other unconditionally, we would be helping each other to manifest those goals as realities. When my turn came, I shared my goals with enthusiasm and joy, drawing energy and support for every word I spoke from that extraordinary assemblage of strong women. Everyone else did the same, declaring boldly what they were bringing into the world—with the exception of one woman. I'll call her Candace.

When Candace's turn came, she spoke enthusiastically about her desires, but in general terms. You could tell she seemed to be holding something back. When our fearless leader and retreat host probed the matter in her nurturing fashion, Candace seemed a little embarrassed and said, "I'm afraid to tell you what it is that I'm hoping for in the sales that I see from my company."

An awkward silence overtook the room. I broke it by asking, "Candace, what is holding you back?"

She had no immediate response. I said, "We have all agreed that what we share here stays here. And we all support you 1,000 percent. Why not share with us the vision for your company?"

It was a fateful question. We talked for a while about what made Candace uncomfortable sharing those numbers with us. I will summarize what she shared with us: Candace had a roadblock. She had a close relationship with a family member whose judgment and disapproval of her had made it hard for her to feel safe celebrating her already monumental success. That history had also made it hard for her to be comfortable talking to *anyone* about what she most wanted to accomplish in her life…even when she knew, on an intellectual level, that she was among people who supported her. Emotionally, she just was not used to speaking about such things out loud. It felt too dangerous.

When Candace finally was able to say her big dream out loud in the context of our group, it had a remarkable effect on her. After just a few minutes of this conversation, I started to see her body language change. She sat up a little straighter. Her gaze was more direct and assured. I could see she was drawing energy from each and every woman in that room. I could tell that it was becoming clearer and clearer to her that we all supported her unconditionally and that none of us would belittle her or criticize her for thinking big.

It struck me at that moment that even someone like Candace, the head of a highly successful company, could be dragged down by the fear of being criticized or ridiculed by other people. This is a potentially paralyzing fear, one to which we are all vulnerable at some point in our lives. But we cannot allow it to hold us back.

We all have ideas. We may fail. But failing doesn't define us as individuals.

If someone you trust tries to tell you the goal that gets you excited is too big, too disruptive, too scary, then guess what? Don't listen to them. They don't really know you. *You* know you. Do what you want to do. It doesn't matter if others can't comprehend your dreams. When they can't—and this is a very important point to hear and understand—they are telling you in that moment what *they* can't do, not what *you* can't do.

> It doesn't matter if others can't comprehend your dreams. When they can't—and this is a very important point to hear and understand—they are telling you in that moment what *they* can't do, not what *you* can't do.

The purpose of that retreat was the same one that led me to write this book: *to empower others and be empowered in turn.* That's why I have been so busy fighting back every fear and doubt for over 40 years. That's why I have spent all those years pressing through whenever I doubted I could make a difference, whenever I doubted I had a story to tell, whenever I doubted my voice was worth hearing, whenever I doubted that I had an aspiration worth pursuing.

But here is the point: we are all like Candace. At our best, we all have a big goal, a dream that stretches us and inspires us, a dream that deserves to be shared…but not with everyone. We have to learn to share our dreams with the *right* people—and to disengage when the wrong people want a say in our lives. That skill of making sure the right people are in our inner circle is not one we are born with. But it is one we can build up over time and eventually master.

As you make your way through the challenges that life reserves exclusively for people of courage, you will notice something important. Not everyone will like you for choosing to meet those challenges. Not everyone will support you for being the kind of person who learns how to keep moving forward. Not everyone will encourage you to learn, grow, thrive, and become all you were meant to be. Lean into the people who do—and away from the people who don't.

DO THIS

Seek out relationships with people who are eager to help you grow and who support you as you learn new things. Minimize your time with people who don't.

Unfortunately, there are going to be people who, for whatever reason, are eager to hold you back and put obstacles in your path. I call them "human roadblocks." Sometimes it will be easy for you to spot them; sometimes it is going to be a little more difficult for you to see these people for what they are. Why? Because that human roadblock may have been part of your life for a good long while. You may have shared a great many experiences with that person. You may even be related to that person. Whether or not you are related to them as family, you are used to looking to them for approval or validation. For these reasons and for any number of other reasons, you may not feel comfortable or happy identifying someone who is currently an important figure in your world as a roadblock.

But if that is what they are, you have to notice. When they show you who they are, believe them.

> "If you believe that your happiness depends on someone else…that belief will undermine all your relationships, including your relationship with yourself."
>
> —Byron Katie

If you *don't feel better* after spending time with a certain individual… if the person spends a great deal of time, effort, and energy *telling you what you can't do*, as opposed to what you can do, and trying to get you to believe in your limitations…if the person, for whatever reason, has some kind of stake in making sure that your status quo *stays* the status quo…if this person sees you becoming your best self as a personal threat…then, make no mistake, you are looking at a human roadblock. This is someone with whom you *must* find a way to limit your time and with whom you *must not* share your dreams. They are taking up valuable space in your life that should be occupied by someone who supports and encourages you.

29. THE CROSSROADS MOMENT

"You are allowed to let go of all those that do not set you free anymore."

—*Dhiman*

I have a friend (I'll call her Rashida) who told me not long ago about the end of a close friendship she'd had with a woman named Dianne. She had known Dianne for many years. Here is her story:

My fiancé Sean had died. He was only 36. I was devastated. If there was ever a time when someone should have been able to count on support from a friend, it was in the days after that horrible loss. I sat down with Dianne right after we had attended Sean's funeral, expecting commiseration, support, and empathy from her—after all, I was the one who was grieving—but instead, all Dianne could do was complain bitterly about her own unsatisfying domestic situation. It was as though my loss hadn't even happened. As far as Dianne was concerned, it hadn't. At one point, she even described her pending divorce as "worse than someone dying." I knew in that moment that I needed distance from Dianne. Up until those words came out of her mouth, I had made excuses for her total lack of support. But when she said that, it became clear to me that I had been participating in something that was not good for me.

There are crossroads moments in each of our lives, moments when we have to evaluate whether people are healthy for us or not. When we come to such a moment, we need to be ready to make brave choices. If somebody doesn't make us feel encouraged or supported, if someone is committed to keeping us from expanding our horizons, then it is time for us to set some boundaries. This is non-negotiable. I am not saying you can't nurture and support the person, but I am saying you must understand the influence they have on you. You must stop seeking personal validation through that relationship. You must stop giving away your power.

We cannot waste our attention, our time, or our energy on anyone who has proven to us that they are committed to holding us back in life or not supporting us. Yes, sometimes it takes courage to make the decision to step away from someone like this. No, it is not always going to be comfortable when we finally step away. But once we have identified someone who meets the criteria of the human roadblock, we *must*.

There are three circles to consider when it comes to establishing the kinds of boundaries I am talking about: *family, people we know,* and *people we have decided to lean into,* meaning people who stretch us. We want to look closely at the best strategies for making brave decisions about each of these groups so that we can claim full agency about the critical issue of whom we do—and don't—spend our precious time, energy, and attention on.

Consider the opportunity cost of maintaining a close friendship with a human roadblock. What could you be doing that you aren't doing because you are stuck in toxic, time-consuming, energy-draining cycles with them? What progress are they keeping you from making on turning your dreams into reality? How much of your time are they eating up? The more time you spend in a negative place with a negative person, the more you will be jeopardizing your future...and your dream.

Ask yourself: *Is this really the best use of my time?*

Ask yourself: *Is this relationship healthy and empowering—or toxic?*

Ask yourself: *Is this relationship making it easier for me to focus on what I can do…or on what I cannot do?*

These are questions only courageous people can take on. Identifying the honest answer may well take us beyond what is comfortable and familiar to us. Once we move beyond that comfort zone, we find our truth and our path. Then we have to speak that truth and follow that path. This is the essence of a crossroads moment.

The first circle we have to consider is your family. There is an old saying among diplomats: "There are some problems for which there are no solutions, only strategic adjustments." One of those strategic adjustments, in the world of diplomacy and statecraft, is the critical, essential decision to set and appropriately defend national boundaries. I believe the same basic principle applies to those family relationships where we are forced to decide what the right thing to do is when one of our close ties is to a family member who is toxic in his or her interactions with us. One of our strategic adjustments has to be a clear decision to set and vigorously defend our *personal* boundaries. Make no mistake—choosing to do this is an act of courage, an act of strength, and a line in the sand we *must* draw if we are to live a bold life, a life rooted in personal integrity.

I do realize that it can be challenging to identify and defend boundaries if your family is one where honoring and respecting those boundaries is not the norm. And I also realize that toxic people, particularly those to whom we happen to be related, can be quite skilled at pulling us into conversations that we don't want to have. The fact of the matter remains, however, that once we claim full agency in our lives, *we* get to decide what treatment we will accept and what treatment we won't. This is true even when (especially when) we are dealing with a close family member.

Here are three things I strongly recommend that you practice saying out loud, in private, or with an accountability partner so that you can say them with confidence and without personal surrender when you are interacting with a toxic family member:

- **"If you don't mind, I'd rather not talk about that."** Repeat this verbatim as many times as necessary. You are under no obligation to share personal information, or any information, with a toxic family member. If they pressure you, say, "Thank you. I appreciate your interest/opinion." Then stop engaging. Say nothing more.

- **"I really can't help you with that."** Toxic family members are good at making their problem look like your problem. Don't let them do that. If you know deep down that you don't want to be part of resolving their latest crisis for them, tell them so directly. You may not be used to doing that, but trust me, you will get better at it with time. Don't ask them questions about the emergency they are facing that they wish would become your emergency. Don't express sympathy beyond a simple one-time acknowledgment along the lines of "I'm sorry you have to deal with that." Look them in the eye and tell them you cannot help. Don't say you wish you could help. Don't offer excuses or justifications about why you can't help. *Just tell them you cannot help them with their problem and then stop talking.* This is not a lack of empathy or care. You are being protective and refusing to be drawn into unhealthy or unproductive drama.

- **"I need to go do X in five minutes (or whatever time limit you choose)."** Set a time limit to the conversation if it is making you uncomfortable but you don't feel you can simply cut it off immediately. Then defend the limit you've set. When the appointed time arrives, *exit the conversation—* because it is your right to establish and defend boundaries about whom you talk to and how long you talk to them.

You do not have to take part in a conversation that does not empower you. Remind the family member that you have a time boundary and that you are asking them to respect it. Whether they respect it or not, *end the conversation and go do what you said you were going to do*. This may feel strange at first if it is not what you are used to doing, but remember: lots of things felt strange to you at first before you did them a few times: delivering a presentation, riding a bike, parallel parking. Setting and defending conversational boundaries is just the same. The more often you do it, the better you will get at it and the more comfortable you will feel when the time comes to do it.

Having looked at your family circle, let's turn now to your circle of friends. You may not be able to choose family, but you definitely can choose your friends. And you know what? You can also *un*-choose them.

There comes a point when you are *obligated* to keep your distance from toxic friendships that are holding you back. I chose that word carefully, and I hope you noticed. If the friendship is toxic, you really are *obligated* to step away from it.

If the person makes you feel bad and exhausts you…if the person is verbally or physically abusive…if the person belittles your goals and ambitions…if the person is controlling and keeps you from expressing yourself…if the person takes advantage of you…*end the friendship*. And prepare for the ride ahead, which may well be bumpy at times.

"When a toxic person can no longer control you, they will try to control how others see you. The misinformation will feel unfair, but stay above it, trusting that other people will eventually see the truth, just like you did."

—Jill Blakeway

You are looking for your personal "Aha!" moment—the moment when you realize on a personal level that a friendship is bringing you down instead of up, the moment when you know for sure that connecting with someone is draining you mentally and emotionally. That moment is the point at which you have an obligation to begin planning your exit strategy.

Years ago, I was flying back from a music festival in New Orleans. On the same flight with me was a woman I'd known for years. We both started our careers in the banking industry. I'll call her Robin. I knew that Robin could be a sweet woman when asked to weigh in on topics that had nothing to do with changing or challenging the status quo—family, current events, holiday preparations, office news—but I had also noticed something troubling: she always had an opinion about something, and that opinion was never positive. She presented her opinions as the voice of reason, but they were really the voice of limitation. She was fun to socialize with, but she always seemed to find the downside of things that were important to me—never the upside. Every time I started to talk about what I really wanted to do with my life, or what she wanted to do with hers, Robin started looking for the smallest, most familiar, most negative, and least risky option possible.

On this particular flight, I told Robin that I was going to be starting a business. When I did, she looked me in the eye and said in a deep and serious tone, "I don't know why in the world you would do something like that, Dee. It's really hard out there. And you *do* have a good job."

I came to two important conclusions about Robin during that flight. First of all, she had never been an entrepreneur, and as far as I could tell she had never tried anything professionally daring—and yet here she was trying to advise me against doing something that she had absolutely no experience in. Second, it occurred to me that although Robin meant well, she was projecting. She was taking her own fears and insecurities and downloading them onto my situation. I'm sure she thought she was being helpful; she might have even felt empowered by expressing an opinion. But what she actually was doing was limiting me with her own way of looking at the world, which was definitely not my way of looking at the world. Here I was, excited and joyful, sharing what I wanted to do with my life, and all Robin wanted to do was to find a way to dial down that excitement and joy. From that day forward, I knew I had to spend less time with Robin. And I certainly never shared my aspirations with her again.

If I had listened to her and others like her, I never would have set my own agenda and pursued my own mission! Thank God I didn't. When I have a problem, I go to the person who has experience in the area in which I am being challenged and who can help me solve that problem. Robin was not that person.

Finding your own path is not easy. You need every bit of love and support and empowerment you can find—and there are lots of people out there who are looking to talk you out of making the most of your life. Very often, their goal is simply to feel superior to you. Is that really the kind of person you want in your life? Why would you want to spend your time with someone eager to get you to focus on what you can't do, as opposed to what you can do? Why would you want to spend your time with someone who is clearly *not* interested in being the light in the room for you?

Here are three big questions I would suggest that you ask yourself about any friendship with someone who reminds you of Robin:

Is it all about them? When you are going through hard times, are they just as committed to being there for you as you are to being there for them? If the support and understanding in this friendship is one-directional, it is not a healthy friendship. Are your friends givers or takers?

When they give you advice, does it come from a place of experience and expertise? Or are they simply projecting their own fears and insecurities and limitations onto your world? Is it possible that the "advice" you are receiving is meant—whether consciously or unconsciously—to keep you from growing and learning and making bigger and better contributions? Is it possible that the prospect of your becoming all *you* can be is unwelcome to this person because they are not yet comfortable with the idea of moving outside of their own comfort zone?

Are they encouraging you to find your own path and learn your own lessons? If this friendship depends on your never making your own decisions and discoveries, it is an unhealthy friendship. Limit the amount of time you spend with people who don't encourage you to grow personally and professionally. And whatever you do, don't make them part of your inner circle.

Here is the bottom line: Our mental state, our happiness, and our overall quality of life is, in very large measure, defined by the quality of relationships we have. Your relationships with others are another secret weapon! They are part of your armor.

Some relationships are healthy for us, while others are toxic, and yet we never seem to do anything about them. That changes today. People in the first two circles who fall into the toxic category get to spend less time with us—or, in extreme cases, no time at all with us. This is the standard that courageous people set and defend.

Now—what about that third circle?

30. THE COURAGE CIRCLE

"Who you spend time with
is who you become."
—Tony Robbins

Early in my entrepreneurial journey, I joined a group called the Runner's Club that changed my life…by helping me to harness the immense power of a special kind of group. Today, I call that group a Courage Circle.

A Courage Circle is a group of people you surround yourself with to help you recognize and achieve what is possible. These are people who constantly remind you of a certain courageous way of living in which learning, contribution, and forward movement are all non-negotiable. They stretch you, they teach you, and they may even make you a little uncomfortable by pushing you beyond your comfort zones. They keep you focused and enthusiastic. They point you toward the best life of which you are capable. Winston Churchill may have captured the essence of this way of living best when he said: "Success is the ability to move from failure to failure with no loss of enthusiasm."[12] The people you put in your Courage Circle inspire you to become the person you were meant to be.

These people empower, stretch, and inspire you. They will say, "Great dream. What if you dreamed even bigger? What if you dreamed even better? Here's how you might do that. Now…what's your next step?"

Here are two true stories that illustrate how a Courage Circle works and why you should enroll yourself in one. Both stories come from my time in the Runner's Club.

The first has to do with a gentleman by the name of Greg White, the program manager of the Runner's Club. Everyone in the Runner's Club took on monthly assignments. One day I was in Florida. I was on vacation, and I was playing golf. There was an assignment due; I had let it slide. My cell phone rang. I checked the number, and it was Greg White.

I answered the phone and said, "Hey, Greg."

Greg was upbeat as always when he said, "Hey, lady. How are you doing today?"

I said, "I'm doing great. What's going on?"

"Well, Dee," he said, "I'm just calling to check in on that assignment. You know, it's due today."

"Honestly, Greg, I am on vacation. I guess I kind of let myself off the hook on that."

It was as though he hadn't even heard that excuse. He continued, positive and upbeat, by asking: "Are you planning on getting it in today?"

I paused only for a second before I heard myself say, "Yes. Yes, of course I am. You know what, I'll have it to you in a couple of hours." I apologized to my golfing partners, left the course, and went up to my hotel room to finish my assignment. I got the assignment done and emailed it to him on time.

This man was there to help me stay the course. How could I let him down by not completing that assignment? How could I let the relationship down? How could I let myself down?

That was my very first experience with having a coach, someone who would hold me accountable for taking steps to achieve a professional goal to which I had committed myself. It certainly wasn't my last. And I learned about that in a Courage Circle.

> When we hold each other accountable, when we expect the best of each other, we fulfill the first rule of a Courage Circle: *we do not let each other off the hook.*

The other story I want to share with you about the Runner's Club has to do with my good friend Carlton Guthrie, a brilliant and successful entrepreneur. He was a strategic advisor of the Runner's Club. Now, there came a point where I was getting very interested in franchising, and I was looking to raise some money. I had put together a business plan for a franchise operation I wanted to start. I asked Carlton to take a look at what I'd done.

Was I ever glad I did! He read through that business plan with as much care and concern as if he had written it himself, and as he talked with me about it, he helped me think about things I'd never thought about. Carlton had many, many notes for me, but I didn't take any of them negatively, because I knew he didn't *mean* any of them negatively. He was there to help me raise my game and elevate my goals.

Carlton was there to help me see what was possible. This was the polar opposite of someone who is critical due to their own insecurity, someone who takes pleasure in shooting down another person's dreams. This was someone who had expertise that I didn't have, looking around every corner on my behalf. Why? Because he was committed to helping me, and others, bring dreams to life in the best possible way. And let me tell you, I was deeply motivated to do the same for him!

I am grateful to everyone in my Courage Circles. There are too many of them to name, but I am blessed to know them all.

> When we look around every corner on someone else's behalf, we fulfill the second rule of a Courage Circle: *we critique and offer insight to help people bring their dreams to life.*

Here is the thing about Courage Circles: we need them just as much as we need the other two circles (family and friends), and sometimes we need them even more. Our mental state, our happiness, and our overall quality of life are, in very large measure, defined by the quality of relationships we have. We need to make sure that we have plenty of quality relationships in this third circle, which may, of course, overlap with both of the other circles. (As I was writing this book, I realized that my mother was definitely part of my Courage Circle!)

Some relationships are healthy for us, while others are toxic, and yet we never seem to do anything about them. Guess what? That changes today. We regularly complete health checks; it's now time for a relationship check.

Starting today, people in the first two circles who fall into the toxic category get to spend less time with you—or in extreme cases, no time at all with you. And starting today, you make a conscious choice to lean into your relationships with people in your Courage Circle. Doing so will help you build the Courage to Hear, the Courage to Dream Big, and the Courage to Do the Right Thing.

DO THIS
Identify someone *right now* who belongs in your Courage Circle.

"IT CAN BE HARD TO LET GO"

It's so important to recognize what our strengths and weaknesses are, because sometimes we're tempted to try to solve every problem. But there are inevitably areas where we're not so strong. We need to know where those areas are for two reasons: so we can work on them over time *and* so we can get help by surrounding ourselves with those who can complete what we can't bring to the table. That's why we want to bring people we trust along with us on our journey. It can be hard to let go. We need people who will gently remind us that sometimes, we think we can deliver perfection, but we really can't.

—Isabelle Freidheim,
founder and chairman of The Board of Athena SPACs

We can always use more relationships where we can both learn and teach, more relationships where we look out for people and be looked out for in turn. We need more relationships where each of us is deeply invested in supporting the other person's growth as a human being. When we have lots of relationships like that, our life becomes more meaningful, we feel happier and more satisfied, and we get better at keeping obstacles and setbacks in perspective. This third circle, the Courage Circle, is all about initiating and sustaining those kinds of relationships. We have to do that *on purpose*. Who will you choose to put in your Courage Circle? How much of your time, energy, and attention will you choose to invest with them this week?

DO THIS

Build your inner circle consciously.

It is quite likely that right now, your inner circle has been designed by default. People stumbled into it. Or you knew them for so long that you assumed they belonged there. Do they?

Make a conscious decision to *design* your inner circle as a Courage Circle. There must be something special about the people you choose to place within this circle. They must be knowledge seekers. They must be solution oriented. As they grow, they must help others grow.

Choose the people you will put in this circle. Make sure they are people who will empower you, support you, encourage you, brainstorm with you, and hold you accountable. Make sure they are people you trust and whose example you would be proud to follow. Make sure they are people who will stretch you and push you to be the very best version of yourself. Once you have an inner circle like that, one that you've designed purposefully, you may just find that it is where the growth and the joy happen most often in your life.

31. BEFORE YOU MOVE ON TO THE NINTH COMMANDMENT, DO THIS

QUESTIONS: COMMANDMENT VIII

- Who in your world is most empowering to you right now? Do you have people around you with whom you feel safe sharing your dreams and aspirations? Your action plans?

- Who would you say is *already* in your Courage Circle right now? Who *could* be in your Courage Circle?

- How much time are you spending on an average day with these people? Do you believe it is worthwhile to spend this time with them? Should this time increase? What can you contribute to each of these people?

- Are you still taking personal private time—time just to be quiet, all by yourself—each day? If not, please re-engage with this commitment before you move on to the next commandment. This is how you build up the Courage to Hear, the Courage to Dream Big, and the Courage to Do the Right Thing.

ACTIONS: COMMANDMENT VIII

- Identify something you can *contribute* to each person you listed who is, or could be, in your Courage Circle. Remember: You are always looking first for something to give back in the Courage Circle. The Courage Circle will never be as strong as it can be if you always have your hand out. In fact, it will never work out if it is approached that way. You must have a learning and giving mindset for this to work.

- Connect with each person on your Courage Circle list. Talk about how you can support each other. Start implementing the best ideas. Seek out opportunities to learn, to push yourselves beyond what is comfortable, to grow.

- Spend more time with the people who make you feel heard and valued and less time with those who don't. Re-evaluate your circles of friends and colleagues. Make the difficult but necessary choices you need to make to empower and enrich your own life.

- Visit www.couragebydesign.com; download, print, and complete the Courage Circle Tool.

Once you have done all this, you will be ready to move on to Commandment IX.

COMMANDMENT IX

Find Success in Failure

"People learn from their failures.
Seldom do they learn
anything from success."
—Ryan Holiday

32. TAKE THE SHOT!

"I've missed more than 9,000 shots in my career. I've lost almost 300 games. Twenty-six times I've been trusted to take the game-winning shot and missed. I've failed over and over and over again in my life. And that is why I succeed."

— *Michael Jordan*

I've lost well over two million dollars on business ideas that didn't work out. Thank God.

That "Thank God" part is vitally important. What's the old saying about missing every shot you don't take? I've taken a whole lot of shots in my life, and just like Wayne Gretzky, who missed over 2,000 shots during NHL games—or Michael Jordan, who famously missed over 9,000 on the NBA court—I've watched as a whole lot of those shots *failed* to put a point on the scoreboard. Thank God I took them, though. Why? Two reasons. First, because I learned something from every shot I missed. And second, because the *act of taking a shot* is what keeps me moving forward in my business and in my life.

To grow my business, I had to learn to step over the fear of failing so I could embrace the *joy* of succeeding. I had to look at the bigger picture—like Gretzky and Jordan and any other highly successful person you choose to name—and see the act of failing as part of the *process* of succeeding. This is something you learn over time. If you don't risk failure by putting a lot out there, nothing big happens. If you don't emulate the winners, who take intelligent chances and try to learn from every outcome, you *can't* put many points on the board.

What I learned from my first business failure—and from all that followed it—is that every decision we make, every setback we experience, every delay we encounter on the way toward the achievement of a worthy goal is an opportunity to identify something important we can learn. Case in point: I opened a restaurant at the Metra station in Chicago because our corporate strategy was to build and operate restaurants and retail stores in high-traffic and captive markets. We had successfully launched in airports. Wasn't the train station high traffic?

When I pulled the trigger on that deal, I ignored a little voice deep inside me that said I was overlooking a couple of important things: the location that was available was too far from the food court that served the people passing by, and the foot traffic peaked during lunch and end of day. At the end of the day, Metra train commuters are only trying to get home. They don't have the long wait times of air passengers. *Details, details,* I thought. *It's the Metra station! Think of the volume of all that foot traffic!*

Not listening to my little voice cost me over half a million dollars. There are any number of other failures I could add to this list. I spent a lot of time, money, and energy on a restaurant concept based on healthy eating choices that just didn't work out. I wanted it to work out, but it didn't. I learned what my mistakes had been, and I kept moving forward.

Now, I can call those experiences "failures," but once I do, I acknowledge, simultaneously, that failure has been my only viable road to success. And by the way, I have never made those mistakes again! I am a lot better now at listening to that little voice, too. Add it all up, and I'm not so sure I didn't *succeed* through experiences like that. Whatever happened, and whatever we call it, *I grew as a person* because of my failures.

> Failure is not a judgment on you as a person. Failure, when followed by informed action, is an important part of the process of succeeding—the part where you learn more about the world and yourself.

Take the best, smartest shot you can. Fail. Fail a lot. When you truly pay attention to what feeds your energy, what sparks you and motivates you, and what is happening in the world around you, you will find that after each failure, you are learning what you need to learn and moving in the direction you are meant to move.

Even when we fail, we still have our innate gifts. The problem arises when we allow fear to cause us to suppress those gifts and keep us from taking shots we really ought to be taking.

DO THIS

Identify the takeaways whenever you fail. For years, you may have heard, or even told yourself, "I'm not good enough" or "I'm not worthy of success" when you fail. Practice SNAP-IT! when you hear yourself thinking that kind of self-destructive thought: snap the band on your wrist and reframe the negative thought to a positive one by asking yourself two questions:

➡ What have I learned?

➡ What can I do differently?

Remember, just because *your idea* failed does not mean *you* are failing. Understanding and living this distinction is what makes the achievement of worthwhile goals possible.

If you are still learning, then *you are succeeding*.

33. FAILURE IS NEVER FATAL

"Success is never final and failure is never fatal.
It's courage that counts."

— *George F. Tilton*

In order to reap the benefits of failure, we need to be able to set aside the question of whether *we* have failed and to focus instead on whether our *tactics* have failed. We need to be able to make the decision to summon *all* our available mental and physical resources and focus our efforts intensely on the task at hand. George F. Tilton, whose words I quoted above, offers a particularly powerful example of this.

Tilton was part of a whaling expedition that got caught in a massive ice pack off Point Barrow, Alaska, in the winter of 1897–98. With the fleet's supplies running low and starvation looming, Third Mate Tilton was chosen to make the long journey to alert the authorities of the disaster—and given 400 pieces of mail to pass along to the US Postal Service. He stuffed his pockets full of crackers and began to improvise his way south, using what he knew about the terrain and what he discovered along the way to make a journey with few parallels in human history.

Tilton walked, sledded, and hitched his way all the way down to San Francisco from Point Barrow, Alaska…and delivered the mail. (The authorities, it turned out, had somehow gotten word of the disaster by then and had already begun a rescue operation.) Tilton had covered more than 1,700 miles over nearly six months in some of the most treacherous and life-threatening conditions on the planet. He encountered freezing temperatures, hunger, and countless other obstacles. He failed innumerable times along the way, as a hunter and in any number of other capacities, due to his being (in his words) "a total stranger to the conditions." Yet *he learned as he went along...and he kept moving forward,* always looking for new ways to close the gap between where he was and where he wanted to be. You and I can do the same.

You may not always hit the target you are aiming for right away. The actions you take and the decisions you make may not always move you closer to the attainment of your goal, but because you can learn from those actions and decisions, adjust to your environment, and courageously move forward, *you will always be exactly what and where you should be.* This is not just Tilton's journey—it's your journey. It is the human journey.

The only way you can fail *as a person* is to decide *not* to learn, not to move forward in a smarter and more focused way than before toward what you are attempting to accomplish. Tilton was right. Success is never final and failure is never fatal...as long as we are willing to learn.

So, pay close attention to what actually caused the failure! Life has a way of sending lessons over and over again until you learn from them. It is up to you to evaluate closely what is working and what is not working in your life. Own that. You may find that what is actually holding you back is quite different from what other people *tell* you is causing the failure, or what you have told yourself in the past is causing the failure.

Get as much good information as you can from as many good sources as you can. Trust, then verify that information. Then move forward, smarter, on new terms.

34. MOVE FORWARD SMARTER

"You can't let your failures define you.
You have to let your failures teach you."

— *Barack Obama*

Let me tell you my favorite story about *moving forward smarter and on new terms*. This story is about a remarkable gentleman named Bill Powell.

Powell, the grandson of slaves, found his great passion in life early on. A caddy at age nine, he became a serious golfer himself in the years that followed. Before long, he emerged as one of the top players on the golf team at Wilberforce University, a historically Black institution in Ohio, my birth state. Suffice to say that by the time Powell went into the military as a young man, he had cultivated a deep love for the sport of golf, and he was very good at it.

During his service in the United States Army Air Forces in World War II, Powell occasionally found the opportunity to play golf on England's courses, which were not segregated. But when he returned home after the war, he found himself in a familiar situation. He was once again banned, like countless other accomplished golfers of color, from all-white golf courses. I will pause briefly here to point out that not only were private golf courses routinely segregated along racial lines during the postwar period, but they *remained* segregated for far too long after that. And while professional sports like baseball, basketball, and football all integrated during the period of the late

1940s to the early 1950s, professional golf remained officially off limits to Black golfers until 1961! Golf was perhaps the last major American sport to get the memo about diversity, equity, and inclusion.

This, then, was the toxic environment to which Powell returned after serving our country during World War II: an environment of stark and unapologetic racism seemingly hardwired into the sport he loved, golf. He did not accept that environment. He decided it was time to change it. He resolved to build his own—unsegregated—golf course.

Like a lot of entrepreneurs, Powell ran into obstacles along the way. Bank after bank refused to finance his business. They told him, in so many words, that his business plan was fatally flawed. Now: Was writing up a business plan, making a formal application, and getting rejected by the banks a failure? I think not. Although Powell had failed to secure the financing he needed in the traditional way, he had not failed as a person. Nor had he given up on his goal. Nor was his business plan the disaster that the banks had made it out to be! Even though he had experienced failure and rejection from one source of financing—namely, the banks—*he kept moving forward.*

"It's distasteful when you get turned down," he once told *The New York Times.* "You have a little pride. You say the hell with them. You say I'm not going to badger. I'm not going to beg them. So I said, *I'll just build a golf course.*"[13]

Meaning, *I'll build a golf course without a bank loan.* Which is exactly what Powell did.

He changed his strategy. He opened his mind to new ideas. He broadened his network. He moved forward a little smarter and on new terms. Eventually, he found two Black physicians who were willing to finance the operation, and he took out a loan from his brother. He then bought a 78-acre dairy farm in East Canton, Ohio, and he set about building the golf course of his dreams...by hand.

Powell and his wife, Marcella, personally moved the boulders, laid down the grass seed, and removed the fence posts. In April of 1948, the first nine holes of the Clearview Golf Club, America's very first integrated golf course, opened to the public. Note that he didn't let the pain of what he had experienced cause him to open an all-Black course! Powell named the course Clearview because he wanted it to reflect his own "clear view" of what the game of golf should be about: access for everyone. That was one part of his business plan that the banks sold short! Today, the course is thriving. It boasts 18 holes and is listed on the National Register of Historic Places.

Powell's daughter Renee, a veteran professional golfer herself and the second Black golfer to play on the LPGA Tour, today serves as Clearview's head golf professional. Of course, she learned the game from her father. She is widely recognized as one of the top golf instructors in the entire country. Powell's son Larry serves as Clearview's course superintendent. Both are actively continuing their father's work and honoring his legacy through the Clearview Legacy Foundation and through PGA REACH, the charitable foundation of the PGA of America.

Stepping into my new role as a trustee of PGA REACH and co-chair of PGA WORKS, the pillar whose mission is to promote more inclusion in the game and diversify the golf industry's workforce, allows me to facilitate the change I hope to see. I know we have to engage in order to expedite the change we want. I know there is much work to be done. The more I engage while working on my golf handicap, the more disparity—and the more opportunity for meaningful change—I witness. I know that, like Bill Powell, we have to make bold, strategic moves to transform setbacks—and shift the paradigm.

Powell's failure to get financing through traditional means led him to success—to a smarter, and legacy-making, strategy for getting his big idea off the ground. Why? Because he was willing to ask himself what was really working and what wasn't; because he was willing to learn and change tactics; and because, like Tilton, he kept moving forward. We need many more soldiers like Tilton, Powell, and Powell's daughter, demonstrating what can be done and what's possible. What change can *you* effect by stepping over failure into a smarter strategy?

"OVER, UNDER, AROUND, OR THROUGH"

My dad was driven. He was absolutely driven to make a difference, to create opportunities, to do something no one had ever done before. And even though there were obstacles that were put before him, obstacles that should not have been there and that would have stopped other people, he dealt with them himself. All of them. He kept going. That was courage for him, and he did teach me that. He said, "You know, everybody has obstacles in life. And the one thing you have to do is to get to the other side; whether you go over, under, around or through, just get to the other side." And I think he did that. He was definitely the leader for me when it came to courage. He was my inspiration when it was my turn to get to the other side. And that day definitely came. I mean, I was on the receiving end of a lot of negative things, including death threats, as a young golfer—because some people didn't want to see a Black woman in professional golf. My courage was to keep going. And my dad was my inspiration.

—Renee Powell,
former American professional golfer and current head golf
professional at Clearview Golf Club

35. GET IN THE GAME

"Get mad, then get over it."

— Colin Powell

My first job out of college was at a bank. I was in a training program designed to foster and develop executive talent. The training program was interesting enough, and it pointed me toward all kinds of useful information. But it didn't take me long to realize that the system that had been set up wasn't exactly putting me on the fast track.

After a few months of keeping my head down, doing my job, and putting into practice everything I was getting from this training program, I couldn't help noticing that a bunch of guys who didn't look like me were the ones who were getting the promotions. I was working just as hard as them, if not harder. They "just happened" to be white, and they "just happened" to be the golfing buddies of some of the senior executives at the bank.

Now, if you are a person of color, one of two things usually happens when you encounter something like this. You notice that a bunch of white guys who go out golfing with the boss "happen" to be getting the plum assignments. The first thing that might happen is you tell yourself, perhaps without even realizing it, that you are to blame, which you aren't. But even though this is not your fault, you might send yourself some variation of the message "I'm not good enough at networking" or even "I'm not good enough," period.

That's not moving forward smarter.

As your coach and ally, I urge you to recognize when you are *internalizing* the failure by judging yourself in this way—and snap that band around your wrist if you find yourself thinking anything like that for even a moment. That's an order!

The second thing that might happen is that you *externalize* the failure by telling yourself that the problem has nothing to do with you but rather with "the system" that is excluding you. You might spend loads of mental and emotional energy obsessing about the shortcomings and bad intent of that "system."

That's not moving forward smarter either.

Let me also encourage you to snap that band around your wrist if you find yourself thinking this! Work your way through it. And once you have snapped the band, remember the wise words of Colin Powell: "Get mad, then get over it!"[14]

In other words, *reclaim your agency*. In this case, you can reclaim your agency by doing what I did: by simply refusing to be an outsider and by getting in the game...by *learning to play golf!*

I'll be honest. Learning to play golf wasn't my first choice for dealing with my situation. I had no interest in golf as a sport, and I would have much preferred if my hard work had been noticed on its merits, without my having to find a way to reach out and make myself more visible. But that wasn't happening. So after I got mad, I got over it.

This was a learning experience. I took on the game of golf as a tactic, a means of engaging with the top people at the bank. At first, that was all it was: a tactic. Initially, it was something I had to do, as opposed to something I enjoyed doing. It was something I felt I needed to do in order to feel included in that environment. It would be years before I would come to love golf for its own sake, as an important part of my life. The more I loved it, the better it worked as a means of connecting with people.

Learning to play golf (badly at first) turned out to be far more important than *anything* I learned in that training program! Golf allowed me to engage with a range of people and say, "Hey, I would love to play with you sometime." It has allowed me to create and expand relationships, to get myself on people's map and get a clearer sense of what is important to them.

Mind you, while at the bank, there was still a gap. I wasn't seeing the top people at the bank with the same frequency as some of the other people in the organization, and I still wasn't a member of the country club (that would come later). But I had overcome a hurdle: the problem of being invisible. I was seeing them. They were seeing me. I was learning from them. So what did I do there? I moved forward smarter. I *noticed what was working for someone else* when it came to rectifying my failure to gain visibility in the bank...and then I *emulated that*. I used a "failure to network" as a stepping-stone to "succeeding at making myself visible."

You can do the same. Ultimately, you play the game for yourself. Find the joy in it as I did, then reap the other benefits.

We're not talking about *winning* the golf game. We're talking about reclaiming your agency. This is far, far better than *internalizing* the failure to create visibility for yourself (by telling yourself that you're not good enough) or *externalizing* the failure (by complaining to anyone who will listen that the system is rigged). Remember what we learned earlier about moving from *solace* to *solution*?

It's true that these environments are not always designed to make people of color feel included. It's true that they are often set up in such a way as to protect the status quo. So the question becomes: *What will you do about that?*

What are other people doing to gain visibility for themselves?

How can you emulate that?

My personal experience is that the golf course is where great personal and professional relationships are built and strengthened; that's become more obvious to me as my own love for the game has deepened. If golf is not in your arsenal when it comes to building and nurturing professional relationships, maybe it should be. I certainly didn't love it at first—I saw it as a tactical response to the failure to fit in at my workplace. But it connected me to people I could learn from, and eventually, to my great surprise, I came to love the game. Who knows? You might come to love it too.

This is a great example of *noticing what is working and what is not working* when it comes to your professional relationships…and then moving forward in a smarter way than you were moving before. This is about claiming your seat at the table and learning from people who can help you—even if they are unaware that their example is serving you.

So, let me ask you: From whom are you learning right now? From whom could you learn?

Let me be very clear about something important: in order to properly address any failure to build and reinforce important professional relationships, *you must make some internal changes first.* You must move beyond the mindset of it being someone else's job to discover you. You must be willing to show up. You must be willing to take the first step. And you must be willing to learn what it takes to *initiate* and *cultivate* relationships. *This is a professional survival skill.*

Yes, mastering that skill takes courage, especially if you have felt shut out from discussions with key people in the past. But courage is the only intelligent response to failure. Every time you start noticing what works for someone else and you start giving what they're doing a try, you are reclaiming your agency. Consider, then, that the failure to create and sustain relationships with people of influence is *your* failure, no one else's. My challenge to you is to courageously *do something about it*—because on the other side of courage, something good is waiting for you.

A SPECIAL NOTE TO WOMEN

Too often, we close doors before they open. Too often, we avoid getting ourselves into the game. I'm not just talking about the game of golf. I'm talking about the game of *life*. It never ceases to amaze me how many accomplished, intelligent professional women find ways to second-guess themselves, to doubt their own greatness, and to miss out on opportunities to connect with *other* women who will support them. And so my challenge to you, if you happen to be a professional woman or if you happen to be a woman who is aspiring to *become* a professional, is to open the door. My challenge to you is to build golf into your life—because this is a choice that opens doors, gets you into the game, and last but not least, surrounds you with women who will support you.

Did you know that Stanford's business school is now requiring women to take golf lessons? Did you know that a study from the research firm Catalyst found that 46 percent of women identified "exclusion from informal networks" as the prime obstacle to reaching important career goals?[15] The study also identified golf as one of those networks.

How do you fix that problem? You get in the game!

Women who learn to play golf tend to fall in love with it. Like me, they may start playing for pragmatic reasons and keep playing it for decades because they love it!

I want to help you open the door. If you are not yet golfing, start! If you are willing to move forward smarter and on new terms, I hope you will connect with us via the PGA REACH website (pgareach.org) so we can talk about how to get you in the game. Or you can email me at dee@couragebydesign.com to ask for more information.

Step outside your comfort zone. Know no bounds. Do not allow fear to keep you from this game's countless rewards! Use your voice, use your power, use your purse to support other women and create more inclusion and equity.

36. BEFORE YOU MOVE ON TO THE TENTH COMMANDMENT, DO THIS

QUESTIONS: COMMANDMENT IX

- Think of the single biggest failure you experienced over the last six months. What happened? What have you learned from that experience? What worked? What didn't work? What do you now know to do differently?

- How can you take what you've learned from this experience and use it to move forward smarter, on new terms?

- Can you see now that failure is not fatal but an opportunity to learn and grow—no matter how embarrassing or awkward it may feel in the moment?

- Are you still taking personal private time—time just to be quiet, all by yourself—each day? If not, please re-engage with this commitment before you move on to the next commandment. This is how you build up the Courage to Hear, the Courage to Dream Big, and the Courage to Do the Right Thing.

ACTION: COMMANDMENT IX

- Find a way *today* to move forward smarter—based on what you just wrote about.

Once you have done all this, you will be ready to move on to Commandment X.

COMMANDMENT X

Your Secret Weapon: Give, Give, and Give Again with Gratitude

"The meaning of life is to find your gift. The purpose of life is to give it away."

— Pablo Picasso

37. START WITH GRATITUDE

"Acknowledging the good that you already have
in life is the foundation of all abundance."
— *Eckhart Tolle*

D o you remember the classic Christmas film *It's a Wonderful Life*? It's one of my personal holiday favorites.

The hero, George Bailey, suffers a series of terrible reverses. Distraught, broke, and believing that his life is meaningless, he considers killing himself—only to have an angel intervene. George sees being prevented from taking his own life as yet another setback. At one point, he mutters to the angel that he wishes he'd never been born.

This remark gives the angel an idea. Suddenly everything changes, and George is brought into a strange and troubling new environment. He finds himself in the world as it would be if he had never been born. In this world, George's beloved hometown has become a sinkhole of drunkenness, crime, greed, and vice…and it is no coincidence that the town is also missing both the affordable housing and the sense of community that George worked so hard to create as head of the local Building and Loan.

In this world, George's wife is a lonely, unhappy woman who doesn't recognize him—and calls the police when he claims to be her husband.

In this world, George's dear uncle Billy has been institutionalized, driven insane by the failure of the Building and Loan, which George was not around to save during the worst days of the Great Depression.

In this world, George's brother Harry perished as a child because George was not there to rescue him from drowning. That means Harry never reached manhood, never joined the military, and thus never saved the lives of hundreds of soldiers who were the target of a suicide bomber. They all died.

George had imagined that his life was pointless, empty, purposeless. But when George's impact on others is removed from the equation, he sees that everything that made a difference to him has diminished and gone dark. In the moment he imagined his life to be meaningless, *he lost sight of the value of his own contributions.* When he sees what the world looks like without them, he begs for his life back.

"You see, George," the angel says, "you really had a wonderful life." Later in the film, the angel leaves George a note that reads: "No man is a failure who has friends."[16] The two lines connect to deliver the point of the film: *Our life has meaning to the degree that we use it to contribute—to establish and support relationships.*

When George is finally returned to his old life, his life has purpose and joy. Why? Because now he is focused 100 percent on giving, on finding new ways to support his relationships with others and contribute. He hugs his wife and family as though his life depended on them—which, of course, it does. Now he is living from a position of profound gratitude for the time that has been allotted to him *to* contribute: to his family, to the town, to anyone and everyone he can think of.

George did lead a wonderful life—because it was a life filled with opportunities to connect through giving. We *all* lead a wonderful life. We all lead lives that touch many, many more people than we imagine. We all have opportunities to create new possibilities and new growth and new connections. In fact, creating those things is what we are here for! We are so quick to obsess about our losses. The only unrecoverable loss, I believe, is the decision not to capitalize on those opportunities to contribute. Our time here is limited. We are meant to use that precious time to *give* in a way that helps others…and thereby help ourselves.

This tenth commandment is about wealth that endures—true wealth. The best and only way to create that kind of wealth, in my experience, is by giving unconditionally and gratefully.

We are not talking here about giving in order to get. We are talking about giving for its own sake, in a way that respects the rights and aspirations of other people and in a way that acknowledges humbly all that *we* have been given, starting with the precious gift of time.

The best advice I can share with you when it comes to fulfilling this commandment is to start where George Bailey started once he got his life back. Start with gratitude. Specifically, be grateful for the present moment. It really is precious.

This moment, right now, is where it all begins. We are talking about using this moment to support the relationship in front of us and the person in front of us, no matter what—because our actual wealth lies, not in our bank account, but in the quality of our relationships. Knowing that makes this moment *huge*. Giving, giving, and giving again, in the present moment, is the key to making our relationships— and our organizations and our societies—work. Not later on. Right now. The most successful people I know are the ones who are totally committed to gratitude for the present moment, for the opportunity to give first in a way that supports, sustains, and empowers others. Now, as you master this commandment, it is your turn to join their ranks.

Ralph Waldo Emerson's famous Law of Compensation states that "Each person is compensated in like manner for that which he or she has contributed."[17] We will always be given back what we have contributed, whatever that happens to be, however vast or tiny that contribution is. And like George Bailey, we have countless opportunities to contribute, countless opportunities to make a difference. But we always begin with the opportunity in front of us right now. And we are always grateful for that opportunity, which always resides in the heart of the present moment.

> "Inch time, foot jewel."
>
> —Zen saying
>
> (Every inch of time is like a foot of precious jewels.)

It is always up to us to use *this precious moment* to make the most of the opportunity to contribute what is most needed to the person who needs it most. No one else can do that for us. We have to do it for ourselves.

So, whom are you here to serve, right now? To connect with, right now? To contribute to, right now?

What relationship will you use this precious moment to improve?

38. A MASTER CLASS IN COURAGE, INTEGRITY, AND SERVICE

"What really pays off in life, I have found, is when you get involved in important things for which you are not paid."

— *Rep. Jim Clyburn*

Recently, I had the high privilege of interviewing a truly remarkable individual, Congressman Jim Clyburn of South Carolina, the current House majority whip, on the topics of courage, integrity, and service. It was an extraordinary conversation, and taking part in it was one of the high points of my career. The highlights appear below.

What was a moment in your life that demanded courage?

Oh, there have been so many, but you know, for some reason I never really think about it until after the fact. Usually, when some situation presents itself, I just sort of act on whatever knowledge I have about it. Then a lot of times I look back and I ask myself, *What made you do that?* And nine times out of ten, it's been the ability to slip into what we call the Prayer of Serenity: *God, grant me the serenity to accept the things I cannot change, courage to change the things I can, and wisdom to know the difference.* You start from the position of wanting to change what can be changed, but I guess you really don't know where the courage part comes into play until you look back. Anyway, I don't.

I can recall the first time I went to jail, after being sentenced for taking part in civil rights protests. The only reason I ever thought of it in courageous terms was the fact that the morning that I woke up in jail, I had a patch of gray hair, which I definitely did not have when I went to sleep. So, you wake up and you look at yourself in the mirror, and you think, *Well, something caused that.* For years, I didn't know what it was. It was only much later that I found out that it was the anxiety and all that went along with it. And only looking back on it like that does it seem courageous. At the time it was just changing what needed to be changed.

I believe what you're talking about when you mention the Serenity Prayer is what I would call integrity, which I believe is a critical component of any meaningful contribution. When you give, you have to give with integrity. Would you say that is what guides you, now that you know that you have more work to do as well?

Well, you know, my dad started training me for leadership from a very early age, I guess from the time I was first born. And we always talked about me following him into the ministry. He wasn't training me for politics; he was really training me for the church. And you mention integrity; my dad used to tell me all the time, "You lead by precept and by example." I can't tell you how many times I've heard him say that to me. And so, I learned early that you must not just say what it is that you're about; you have to demonstrate it time and time again. And I guess he knew that in particular contexts, it takes a lot of courage to express a particular precept, to make sure it gets demonstrated. And so, yes, I grew up with that. And I still live by that to this day. And yes, this is about integrity, sure. You know, this is one of the reasons I'm having real problems trying to understand what's going on in the country today, because in the past, even when people did not practice integrity, they were always of the opinion that there ought to *be* real integrity in public service. And somehow that has changed for a lot of people.

How has it changed?

In the past, even if people in public service were not genuine, you could look at what they'd said and you could say, "Well, that's hypocrisy." You know, at least the hypocrisy was there! Today, a lot of people don't even bother with hypocrisy. They just lie. They don't even bother trying to look like they're telling the truth anymore. And so you've got to wonder, when you start missing hypocrisy, isn't truth one of those precepts that my dad talked about? Isn't that the part of the glue that is supposed to hold us together? Where are those precepts? For a lot of people in public service, and a lot of people in the media, and a lot of people in other walks of life, there's not even the precepts, much less any personal example of living them.

What kinds of courageous acts would help to address the problem you're talking about?

Speaking up. Another thing my dad said to me all the time was "Silence gives consent." To remain silent is to consent. Now, Martin Luther King, Jr., said it a different way. In his letter from the Birmingham City Jail, King wrote that he was coming to the conclusion that the people of ill will in our society were making a much better use of their time than people of goodwill. And he also said that people were going to be made to repent, not just for the vitriolic words and deeds of the people of ill will, but for the appalling silence of good people. And so I think that what we have experienced today is that too many people prefer to be silent when they see so much going on around them that requires speaking up. We tend to make excuses for not saying anything, not getting involved. That, to me, is a very, very dangerous situation, just to pretend that because I didn't do it, or I didn't say it, I have no responsibility for it. We must use our voices.

This part of the book is about giving. I believe one of the most important forms of giving is public service. How would you define public service? And how would you propose that we get more young people to think about that kind of service?

Public service is just what it is: serving the public. The name tells you all you need to know. This is public. It is not private; it's not personal. It's the public good. So in my memoirs, I close with an open letter. The epilogue of that book is an open letter to my children, to my grandchildren, and to all the other children similarly situated. And what I say to them is that if you plan to go into business, you should get to know the people you want to sell your goods and services to. To me, those relationships are just as important as the goods and services that you have. You have to get to know those people. Now, if you want to go into public life, the same principle applies. You need to get to know the people that you want to devote your service to, the people whose lives you are going to affect. The big mistake that I see young people making in this area is that they focus on how to make themselves acceptable. They seem to be thinking, *You've got to get to know me; you need to know who I am.* No. First, *you* find out who *they* are. You find out what *you* can do to help them fulfill their dreams and aspirations. And if you do that, the other stuff will take care of itself. So when it comes to public service, I think that we have to be willing to make it about the public and not about us. And if you think about it, that's the big, big problem that's going on today.

It sounds like you're saying that what distinguishes a generous public servant from an ungenerous one is the ability to set all of the self-interest aside—every bit of it. Am I right?

Absolutely. And self-interest, to me, is the worst reason to be in public service. If you're doing it to aggrandize yourself, you're in this line of work for the wrong reason. You know, I was speaking to a reporter earlier today who had heard that I had stepped aside on a commencement address that I had been scheduled to give at South Carolina State University. The reporter asked, "Why would you give up doing the commencement address?" I said, "Because it's going to be more meaningful to the students to hear from the president of the United States than it is going to be for them to hear from me." Listen, I'm a graduate. They can see me all the time. But if they have the chance to hear from the president, that's an experience they are not going to have otherwise. So I reached out to the White House. And he's going to do it. My whole thing is, it's about them. It's about providing them with an opportunity to grow and giving them something to remember. They will remember for years to come that a president came and spoke to them.

Do you think that is the kind of thing that might encourage young people to go into public service?

Absolutely. And understand, public service does not just mean running for office. Public service is something we all need to do at some point. I say all the time, "Find something to do for which you're not paid." And I say that to young people especially, and especially during commencement addresses. If you're only doing something that you're paid to do, there's something important missing. What really pays off in life, I have found, is when you get involved in important things for which you are not paid. And you know what? People see you making a contribution that way, and they reward that. And the rewards come much more quickly for that than it does for those things that you're paid to do.

What else are you likely to tell young people during a commencement address?

Don't give up. Don't give up. Don't give up. And remember that the first sign of a good education is good manners. Never forget to say, "Thank you." That, to me, is very, very important.

It sounds like you're saying that civility is at the core of public service.

Absolutely. And we've gotten away from that. Just look how far we've gotten from that. And we wonder why things are going so awry.

Civility is another one of those precepts: we need to teach it, and we also need to live the example. And so often that's just gone by the wayside. The country is in transition on so many fronts, and I think one big reason civility often doesn't figure into the equation has to do with changes in the way we communicate. When I was coming along, you had to engage with people face to face; you had to interact with people in person. And civility was part of that. It was expected. Yet so many people today are all about, "Is it a sound bite? How many people follow your sound bites? How many hits did you get?" That is not an environment that reinforces civility. Today, a lot of people are all about headlines rather than headway. I still subscribe to the notion that you ought to be in public service to make headway. But I know this: too much today is about who makes the headline. And so, in this kind of transition, I think people are eventually going to find a way to work through this, but right now, the headlines are winning.

How can people in the private sector make headway?

Well, you know, it's all about taking a risk for what you believe. You've got to take a stand and you've got to take risks sometimes. You've got to have the courage to take a risk if you want to succeed. That's not to say that you have to be reckless to take a risk. But you can't isolate yourself, especially if you're trying to build a company. I mean, you take a risk when you walk out your front door. So you've got to go out and say, "I know there's a chance that this may not work, but there's also a chance that it might. So I'm going to do this," because if you wait until all the conditions are perfect, you never make a contribution to anyone.

My mom had a powerful way of saying that. She told me one time, right after our first child was born, "You've got a family now. You need to buy a house and make a home for your family." We were living in an apartment at the time. And I said to her, "Yeah, Mama, I'll do that, just as soon as I can see my way clear." She looked me in the eye, and she said, "Son, let me tell you something: if you wait until you can see your way clear before you attempt anything, you'll never get anything done." She was right. And I think my dad would have referred me to the book of Hebrews, the eleventh chapter, the first verse, where it says, "Faith is the substance of things hoped for and the evidence of things unseen." You have to strike out on faith. So that's what I would tell people in the private sector: Be bold. Strike out on faith.

39. THE GIVING PRINCIPLE

"Life's persistent and most urgent question is,
'What are you doing for others?'"

— *Martin Luther King, Jr.*

My mom made a big deal out of Sunday dinners. Sunday evenings were her masterpiece. I've already told you that she was all about leaving people and places better than she found them and that she instilled that same deep purpose in each of her kids. But what I haven't shared was how central food in general, and Sunday dinner in particular, was to Mom's plan for making that improvement of people and places *happen* on a regular basis. If you were lucky enough to be around when it was time to take a seat at my mom's Sunday evening dinner table, you learned (or relearned) what it meant to be loved, taken care of, and nourished—not just physically nourished, but emotionally and spiritually. Although she never earned an advanced degree from any fancy university, she had a PhD when it came to giving, and Sunday evening was when class was in session. Even in meager times, Helen Hill somehow found a way to take care of everyone at that time.

Gratitude and giving back were the laws my mom lived by. The first group of people she wanted to give to was always her kids, but the giving did not stop with us. She wanted to change the world *through* her kids, so she never stopped trying to instill that high sense of purpose in us, and she never stopped encouraging us to learn, to explore, to develop our talents and capacities. That's what Sunday evenings were all about for us as a family. When we were facing an obstacle or a challenge, Sunday dinner gave us a boost and made us feel we would soon find a way to overcome it, no matter how daunting it might have seemed. When we had a dream about something we wanted to do with our lives, Sunday dinner was the time when we could share that and be supported in making it a reality.

At one level, of course, the Sunday gathering was all about the meal she had prepared for us: oven-fried chicken, to-die-for cornbread, sweet potato pie, pound cake—my mom had a lot of options. But at a deeper level, Sunday dinner was about recharging us all, settling love into our lives, letting us know that she knew we could fight the good fight and make the world a little better. Her Sunday dinners engendered love. They embodied warmth. And thanks to her personal example, they modeled and inspired hard work.

I believe my mom was at her best when she was preparing and sharing that Sunday dinner, and I think that was because she radiated the joy of giving back. Whenever I think of those times with her, I'm reminded about why she was, and is, my hero. The meals she prepared for us and shared on those precious evenings meant so much to me and had such an impact on me as both a daughter and as an entrepreneur that I was eventually inspired to honor her legacy by collecting them in a cookbook, *Stirring Up Good Trouble: Food for Thought, Food for the Soul.* And of course, it's no coincidence that my mom's legacy of leaving people and places better than she found them by means of the communal gift of sharing food has become the centerpiece of my career and my company, Robinson Hill.

Everything I do now, including running a successful company, writing that cookbook, and writing this book, is an attempt to live up to, and extend, my mother's powerful example when it came to giving. She gave to her family, not as a tactic for personal gain, but *as a way of life.* In fact, I would say she aimed to give something to everyone she touched or came in contact with, which was one of the reasons so many people loved her. And she gave, through us and through her own efforts, to the generations to come, because she knew that countless people before her had done the same thing on her behalf, some without even knowing her. She knew there was a special group of people who find a way to give that simultaneously helps move those they care about, and society as a whole, forward *in the long term.* She wanted to be one of those people. And she wanted each of her kids to be one of those people, too.

No matter how we felt when we sat down to Sunday dinner, no matter what we had been dealing with during the week, we always knew that when we got up from the table, we'd have full bellies, soothed spirits, warmed hearts, and the strength to fight the good fight. That was her gift to us, and it was invaluable.

I call the idea of giving as a way of life, like my mother did, the Giving Principle. Fulfilling the Giving Principle is all about creating and executing a plan to give something that you yourself would like to receive and doing so in a way that accomplishes three vitally important goals:

- Helping a specific person or group of people in a tangible way *today*
- Helping those same people aspire to do, be, and become more *tomorrow*
- Helping society as a whole

This kind of giving turns you into a catalyst for good, just like my mom was, by connecting you to something larger than yourself.

The Giving Principle is not to be confused with giving in order to get something in return. It is unconditional giving that uplifts people you care about, people in need and people yet unborn. It is the kind of giving that pays forward the *idea and practice* of giving to a new generation of givers.

Let's be honest with ourselves: this kind of giving does not come naturally or easily. It takes commitment and a sense of personal purpose. It takes practice, and it takes courage. But once that courage takes root in the form of consistent action, we create better habits. And when we create better habits, we create a better life for everyone. We have to teach ourselves to live like that!

Yet most of us have been taught *not* to give unconditionally. We want something for ourselves first. Before we put ourselves out there, we expect signs of a clear and immediate return on our "investment." Note the quote marks there: unfortunately, cynicism, self-interest, and short-term thinking too often destroy any possible return for anyone in the relationship. Because of our deeply ingrained habit of maintaining a self-focused attitude, we usually *don't* think about giving unconditionally. Most of us *don't* walk into a room full of strangers and start looking for something we can do that will help one or more of those people in a tangible way today, inspire them tomorrow, and move all of humanity forward in the weeks, months, years, and decades ahead.

Yet that is what this commandment challenges us to do—as one of the guiding principles of our lives. *Give, give, and give again.* That doesn't mean we let people take advantage of us. It means we choose not to let anyone change who we are; and wherever we go, whatever we do, we strive to plant seeds of giving, seeds that will bloom and bloom and keep blooming so they can be of genuine benefit…for generations to come.

Notice that my mom's tradition of Sunday evening dinners meets that challenge. It checks all three of those boxes I mentioned.

1) It helped her kids on the day it happened. I know because I was one of those kids and I was there.

2) It strengthened us and inspired us to pursue our dreams in the days and weeks ahead. I know it did that, too, because those dinners were a huge part of what inspired me to pursue the path of entrepreneurship and, eventually, to build a company.

3) It made us better people by inspiring us to continue and honor the example of giving with which our mom had inspired us. It was our armor for the week to come. Her mission was to support us emotionally and every other way she could. Today, I not only share my own version of my mom's Sunday evening dinners with my own family; I also live her example every day by pursuing my own mission:

To use my voice and example to help others and shorten the runway to success, to empower people and organizations to overcome fears and limitations, and to elevate their thinking about what is possible.

Today, when I sit down with my daughter, or walk into a meeting, or join a party, or give an address, or sit down for a coaching session, I see someone who can help me fulfill that mission, someone who can join forces with me in making it a reality. I see myself in them, and I see opportunities to give. And when I connect with young people, particularly young women or young people of color, I am all about finding ways to give that will shorten the runway to success for them and help them to find their own mission, their own purpose, and their own path. And every time I move forward on my mission, whether that's in a big way or a small way, I know that progress connects back to what my mom so freely gave us during those Sunday evening dinners: total unconditional support and love.

Your task now is to make the Giving Principle a practical, ongoing reality in *your* life, just as my mom made it a reality in hers and, eventually, in mine. Your task is to identify a relationship that really matters to you—professional or personal—and set up a plan for putting far more into that relationship than the other person expects from you. Serve them Sunday dinner.

> **DO THIS**
>
> Identify a relationship that really matters to you—professional or personal—and set up a long-term plan for putting far more into that relationship than the other person expects from you. Then... execute that plan.

Set aside any grievances. Let God sort those out. Set aside what you feel you deserve. Let God sort that out too. If the relationship is important to you, your job is simply to give, give, and give again, so powerfully and so consistently that your giving inspires others to do the same. Your bounty will come of its own accord, not because of any scores you settle or vindication you demand. Just give.

DO THIS

Give. Be a part of changing things in the world for the better. Do it for those you love: your children, parents, grandparents, or those ahead. Give as those before you gave to move your world and your opportunities forward. Don't ignore the struggles, pain, sacrifices, and lives lost on your behalf. Don't disrespect those on whose shoulders you are standing. Give. Pay it forward. Don't rob the world, or yourself, of your contributions. Claim and acknowledge the only real power you have. Don't make it about the money. Make it about giving.

"I refuse to accept the view that mankind is so tragically bound to the starless midnight of racism and war that the bright daybreak of peace and brotherhood can never become a reality.... I believe that unarmed truth and unconditional love will have the final word."

—Martin Luther King, Jr.

40. BEFORE YOU MOVE ON TO THE ELEVENTH COMMANDMENT, DO THIS

QUESTIONS: COMMANDMENT X

- Whom do you leave better than you found them? Whose life are you influencing? Whom are you serving right now? Whom can you serve? How could you serve them—or serve them better?

- Do you have a giving mindset? When you meet someone new, is your first thought about how they can help you—or about how you can help them?

- What kind of giving gives you joy? How can you give more of that?

- Do you regularly invest in people by considering how you can help them and reaching out to see how you can add value to their lives without needing something in return?

ACTIONS: COMMANDMENT X

- Accept that you have the power to influence lives for the better. Reclaim the agency of giving and influence.

- Don't let a "taking" mentality rob you of the chance to contribute. Let the universe take care of the compensation. Invest in someone outside your family circle. Do this by reaching out to support them without expecting anything in return.

- Are you still taking personal private time—time just to be quiet, all by yourself—each day? If not, please re-engage with this commitment before you move on to the next commandment. This is how you build up the Courage to Hear, the Courage to Dream Big, and the Courage to Do the Right Thing.

Once you have done all this, you will be ready to move on to Commandment XI.

COMMANDMENT XI

Win the Race: Make Good Trouble by Putting Your Heart and Soul into Diversity, Equity, and Inclusion

"Not everything that is faced can be changed, but nothing can be changed until it is faced."

—James Baldwin

41. SILENCE IS NOT AN OPTION

"In the end, as any successful teacher will tell you, you can only teach the things that you are. If we practice racism, then it is racism we teach."

— *Max Lerner*

My *purpose* in life is to leave people and places better than I found them. My *mission*, which is my purpose in action, is as follows:

To use my voice and example to help others and shorten the runway to success, to empower people and organizations to overcome fears and limitations, and to elevate their thinking about what is possible.

Note the word *voice.* Fulfilling this mission means speaking up, and specifically it means using my voice to take on the biggest and most lethal dragon of them all: prejudice that demeans, excludes, and limits human potential. Why do I call prejudice the biggest dragon of them all? Because it has the power to diminish and degrade not only our organizations, but ourselves and our entire society as well. And if leaders of all colors, all sexual orientations, and all walks of life do not step up, start the difficult conversations, listen to what comes back, and find a way to slay that dragon, we are all in deep trouble. In fact, we *are* in deep trouble, but we can find a way out. By making good trouble.

I happened to be at a recent business meeting when one of the executives preparing to make a presentation referred to those of us present—his superiors—as "guys and girls." Now, I know any number of men, and women, who might be comfortable being referred to as "guys" in a business meeting by a subordinate, but I don't know any who would be comfortable being called "boys." Not one. Yet here he was calling the only three women, who all happen to be senior management, "girls." It was startlingly inappropriate, and the moment he said that, I knew I had to intervene.

I said, "Excuse me—no, not girls."

He stammered, muttered an apology, then got back to his presentation. It was an awkward moment, but sometimes that is the only way to dismantle the status quo.

There were about a dozen men in the room that day, and three women. Perhaps this person was used to working in rooms where women were either not present or, if they were present, they were unwilling to cause an awkward moment. I am not that kind of woman. Seriously: If you were lucky enough to schedule a meeting with Bill Gates, Elon Musk, and Jeff Bezos, and you were there to make a presentation to them, are there *any* circumstances under which you would call them "boys"? I don't think so.

I knew that by speaking up, I was speaking up, not just for me, but for everyone in the room, for every woman in the organization. Was I overreacting or reading too much into it? I don't think so. His comfort with such a term suggests something pervasive, something that needs to be addressed directly.

Think for a moment about what would have happened if I hadn't said what I said. When we don't speak up in the moment, we lose the *power* of the moment. We lose our agency. We start to stew about what happened, which isn't helpful. We start replaying the exchange over and over again in our heads, thinking about what we could or should have said. That's not helpful either. And perhaps most importantly, *we do not change the behavior on the ground.* In fact, we reinforce it by letting our silence imply that we are okay with it when we're not. That means the marginalizing behavior is likely to continue. That means we are part of the problem. We don't want to be part of the problem. We want to be part of the solution.

Yes, I made the room a little uncomfortable for a moment. But do you know what else I did? I brought a heightened awareness to what had happened to everyone in that meeting. And I made sure that the gentleman who had diminished and marginalized us didn't do it again!

Let me share another powerful true story from Monica Cole, who serves as a senior executive at a major American bank. What Monica has to say is important to your courageous journey whether you are a white person or a person of color; whether you are male, female, or other; whether you are straight, gay, or other. What she has to say is important to your journey as a *human*. I'll let Monica take it from here.

"THIS IS BAD"

Early on in my career as a lender, I had agreed to a dinner meeting with one of the most prominent CEOs in the Southeast, a customer of mine. This was an important meeting for our bank. My manager, I knew, would be in attendance at this dinner. He had scheduled it in a private room at one of the oldest and most exclusive country clubs in Atlanta. I didn't know anything about the country club I was going to. I did know about its reputation, though.

Once I arrived at the right address, I realized that I had

no idea where the entrance to this country club was. No one had bothered to tell me how to get in. I was assuming it would be obvious, but it wasn't. My boss and the CEO had been there multiple times, so they obviously knew exactly where to go. But I didn't.

So I finally made my way in, and I was looking for help, trying to figure out where I was supposed to be. After a while, I ran into a woman who worked at the country club who directed me to where this private event was being held. So I followed her directions, and I walked toward that private room; and as I walked, I was looking all around me, monitoring the situation closely for my own safety—which is what you learn to do from a very young age as a person of color when you enter an unfamiliar social environment. (It's called "tracking.")

Suddenly I am seeing what is happening here: white men and women and white families are having dinner and drinking and socializing, without a care in the world—and at the same time, I'm seeing Black people serve them. Every single person on the country club's support staff is Black. And I'm thinking to myself, *This is bad.*

And then I walk into this private room, the exclusive room where my customer is and where my manager is, and the exact same thing is happening: white people in charge, Black people serving them. My head is spinning. I just am not emotionally prepared for what I am walking into. I have to take a deep breath after I sit down just to calm myself. I'm being asked to perform as a professional in my role as a lender, while having to process the reality of being in a social environment like that. I have to conduct myself professionally under those conditions.

I decide not to say anything about what I am going through. It is a difficult decision, but since I am representing my company and I am responsible for sustaining this relationship with this important customer, I choose to conduct myself accordingly. I pretend as though what is happening around me is not happening…because my customer and my manager are each acting as though nothing is happening.

What is increasingly clear to me, though, as the dinner meeting proceeds, is that I am now in a room with people who look like me who are being treated as servants. And I feel complicit with that. And it's not good. Clearly I am part of an establishment that from my perspective, routinely views people who look like me in a servant role.

Fast forward. Later that year, I go to that same manager's house for a holiday party, a Christmas party.

I show up at the address and I ring the doorbell, and a Black woman answers the door. She is dressed in what appears to me to be a 1950s housemaid outfit.

And my head starts spinning again.

She says, "May I take your coat?"

I said, "No, ma'am, I will not be here long."

And it is at that moment I know my career doesn't matter over my dignity.

I walk into that house and find my manager—in a room filled with my coworkers. I look him in the eye, and I say to him, "I just want you to know, I came. And now I'm leaving."

Me saying that to him is the talk of the office the next day. The only person with enough courage to ask me about that moment, though, is the Black administrative assistant who works for my manager.

She comes over to my desk and says, "I heard something happened last night." And I tell her exactly what happened and how I felt and why I said what I said. Then I tell her, "If anyone wants to talk about it, they know where I'm sitting." There comes a moment in time when you realize, "I don't have to take this crap." Because you know what? You don't. I mean, this was 1998, and here he was, decking this woman out like it was 1950. So it was the same cycle, the same dynamic, as what I had experienced at the country club. But the setting had changed. This was not me representing the company in front of a customer. This was not a professional event. This was private time—my time. And I knew, the minute I saw that maid outfit, that I was not prepared to socialize in that environment. So I had no problem saying so, right out loud. And no problem leaving.

The next year, that same manager's Christmas party still had the same Black woman opening the door and taking coats. But her maid's outfit had been replaced by a simple black blouse and black pants. So that was progress.

—Monica Cole,
senior bank executive

Speaking up in a situation like that requires courage. Listening requires courage too. Taking action to change the assumptions and the outcomes also requires courage. What Monica was dealing with—what so many of us have to deal with on a daily basis—is the reality of an inequity that is deeply, deeply rooted in the status quo, inequity that has taken up residence in that tired phrase "But we've always done it that way."

Here's the insidious thing about discrimination: *it usually doesn't feel like discrimination to the people who are engaging in it.* It feels like the status quo. It feels like "what we have always done here." It feels familiar. That familiarity is a curse because it constitutes a major obstacle to organizational growth and performance. That curse needs to be reversed. The means by which we overcome that curse is by building the courage to speak up for progress in three different areas:

DIVERSITY: Does our team represent the larger world?

EQUITY: Does each individual on our team have the tools needed to access resources and opportunities? Equity is not the same as equality. My favorite example of this is: *Equality means everyone has a pair of shoes; equity means everyone has a pair of shoes that fits.*

INCLUSION: Does everyone on our team feel emotionally and psychologically safe? Does everyone on our team feel heard?

Monica's decision to speak up for diversity changed the status quo, and that's not always easy or comfortable for those impacted by the change. If you're the manager in that story, it might be easy for you to think to yourself: *What's the problem here? We've always used this country club for important meetings with key decision-makers.* Or: *What's the problem here? I don't have any control over how the country club hires its staff.* Or: *What's the problem here? People have been wearing that uniform in my house for years.*

But even though it would be easy to respond in these ways, *it would not be right.*

Why not? Because sometimes the status quo, as designed, is hurting people.

The fact that we have always done it that way does not mean that it is right. For instance, "We've always done it that way" means that someone who is used to thinking of people of color as "hired help" feels no hesitation about casually approaching *all* people of color who happen to be unknown to them as though they were "hired help." As someone who has frequently been mistaken for "the help" at any number of public gatherings, including many at which I was a scheduled speaker, I can tell you that this kind of thing has an impact. Silence is not an option. We have an obligation to find a way to respond that sustains our dignity, maintains a professional environment, and helps us to move the relationship forward. ("I'm sorry, but you're mistaken. I'm one of the presenters.")

"We've always done it that way" means that someone who has, for whatever reason, grown used to thinking of women or people of color as subservient at home or in the workplace will often use language and make decisions that betray that assumption. These kinds of slights are worth speaking up about. They are so pervasive for people of color, for women, and for those whose gender and/or sexual orientation are not considered traditional that it may be difficult for people who are not in those groups to grasp just how demeaning and disempowering they can be. I tell people that the experience is like having a woodpecker perched on your shoulder, tapping away night and day. It literally never stops. That's the reality of "We've always done it that way."

That woodpecker can either sap the human spirit or inspire it to great acts of courage. The choice is ours. I chose the latter. Monica chose the latter. And now it is your turn.

I want you to choose to make the most courageous professional choice you can make, personally and organizationally: the choice to move beyond your current comfort zone on the issue of diversity, the choice to start difficult conversations with people who don't look or sound like us and then setting new priorities based on what we hear back.

Most leaders—let's face it, most human beings—fail that test. Silence is easy. "We've always done it that way" has been used to create silence and justify inequity on both the large and small scales for as long as humans have occupied this earth. It is only the courage of individual human beings choosing to speak their truth, tactfully but unmistakably, and choosing to back up their words with bold actions that has ever managed to turn those inequities around and make them opportunities for growth on both sides of the conversation.

There are times when the status quo is broken and it has to be fixed. Period. George Floyd and countless others paid with their lives to teach us that. And if you have made it through the earlier chapters of this book to reach this chapter with me, I believe you are one of the people tasked with doing the fixing—no matter your color, your gender, or your sexual orientation. Like Monica, you will at some point find yourself face to face with a status quo that is hurting people. You will find yourself in a situation where the basic, authentic, impossible-to-sugarcoat human response is "Enough already." And at such moments, I want you to know that you have the duty, and the privilege, of speaking up appropriately for what is right. Some people will see this as making trouble. In fact, it is what Congressman John Lewis used to call "good trouble." And we need people to make more of it. If not now, then when?

> "[We are] through with tokenism, through with gradualism, through with see-how-far-you've-come-ism. [We are] determined now to gain these basic rights which have been guaranteed by the Constitution, God-given rights, and yet they have not been carried out."
>
> —Martin Luther King, Jr.

Your purpose and *your* mission must inspire you to become one of those courageous human beings who speaks up courageously whenever you encounter inequity. This is the race we must run…and win.

42. YOUR PURPOSE, YOUR MISSION, YOUR VALUES

"It is in your hands to create a
better world for all who live in it."
— *Nelson Mandela*

I believe that if you are living a life whose core principles have been designed courageously, then diversity, equity, and inclusion are woven right into your DNA. Fulfilling those principles must be an integral part of who you are: an intrinsic part of living your own purpose, pursuing your own mission, and making the best possible decisions based on your own values. That's the only way those principles can ever translate into a personal and organizational advantage.

What we are talking about here cannot be pasted on from the outside. It must be lived authentically from the inside out. A perfect example of that in my own life came about a few years ago, when I had to make one of the toughest decisions of my career.

We had hired a senior accounting and finance executive I'll call Michelle. Now, Michelle was extraordinarily talented, and she delivered really remarkable results. But she had a temper, and she lost a number of very good managers because of her communication style, which could be abrupt, aggressive, and abrasive.

Now, at Robinson Hill, we have a list of core values that we live by. Among those values are INTEGRITY (meaning we do the right thing whether someone is watching us or not) and RESPECT (meaning we do not put ourselves above other people; we are all valued). Those aren't the only values, but they're the ones that are most relevant to this story, so those are the ones that I'm sharing with you.

There came a point where I had to do what I like to call a "mirror check." I had to confirm that I was staying true to the purpose, the mission, and the values I had laid out for myself and the organization. Specifically, I had to make sure I was acting with INTEGRITY and upholding the value of RESPECT for myself and others in my organization.

And after my personal "mirror check," I had to admit to myself that I had been so impressed with the financial results Michelle had been delivering that I had been minimizing her failure to live the Robinson Hill values. And it *was* a failure. I was failing in that area. The fact that good people who reported to Michelle kept leaving the company should have tipped me off to that fact long before I received word that she was showing unacceptable favoritism. That's not how we operate at my company.

Even if I hadn't gotten those reports, though, I could not have ignored a clear pattern that had emerged and repeated itself for several years. The pattern looked like this: Michelle losing her temper, treating people disrespectfully; Michelle apologizing when I called her on it and refusing coaching; Michelle appearing to live the values but only acting in accordance with them when I was around, as compared to when I wasn't. Then the cycle began all over again, escalating in the process.

It was an unhealthy cycle. To ignore it was to paper over the truth. And the truth was, Michelle was either unwilling or unable to live the company values.

This wasn't just a matter of *Michelle* not operating with INTEGRITY and not upholding the value of RESPECT. As long as I was facilitating and enabling her behavior, *I* was not living those values either! And no diversity, equity, and inclusion initiative at Robinson Hill, or anywhere else, is possible without INTEGRITY and RESPECT from the top.

I let her go. That was not an easy decision, but it was the right decision. And not only was *I* glad I had made that decision—the whole organization was glad I had!

> "Cultural diversity brings a collective strength that can benefit all of humanity."
>
> —Robert Alan

Let me tell you about my dear friend Jim Lowry. Jim is an unstoppable force. He is also a business icon; a seasoned, highly successful consultant and entrepreneur; and the author of the magnificent book *Change Agent: A Life Dedicated to Creating Wealth for Minorities*. His memoir's title says everything that needs to be said about his personal mission.

Jim holds the distinction of being the first African American consultant ever hired by the elite firm McKinsey & Company. That was back in the late 1960s, a tumultuous chapter in American history with many parallels to the extraordinary period that America—and the world—has had to navigate in the early 2020s. I asked Jim to share some of the lessons he picked up as a young man about courage and mission orientation on a personal level—lessons that could be shared with young people facing similar challenges. This is what he had to say:

> *It was certainly an interesting time. Sometimes people would call you "Uncle Tom" and so on. People love to talk, so they would say things like, "I hear he works for this company called McKinsey on Park Avenue now. Why did he want to*

leave Bedford-Stuyvesant? Does he think he's some kind of local hero now that he decided to go to Wall Street?" And of course, that was on top of everything that I was dealing with at work. So really, the static was coming at me from multiple directions. And I think the advice I give younger people about that kind of thing is actually pretty simple: if you know where you want to end up, you'll be all right.

Sometimes you have to make certain moves in your life, and that's fine…as long as you know where you want to go. And sometimes, when you're going where you know that you need to go, you have to learn how to flinch and stay on track—because make no mistake, you are going to get static. You'll get static from your people, and you'll get static from other people. But that static shouldn't deter you from where you ultimately see yourself going and the impact you want to have on your society. So you sometimes just have to turn the other cheek. For my part, I knew I wasn't just in it for myself.

I often found myself thinking of that famous discussion between Branch Rickey and Jackie Robinson, when they were laying the groundwork for integrating Major League Baseball back in the late '40s. Branch Rickey asked Robinson to come to Brooklyn and talk things over. Their conversation went on for a long time, and one of the things they discovered is that they were both committed to the same mission, and it wasn't just about baseball. That mission had a personal and a spiritual dimension for both men. At one point, Rickey said, "Well, Jackie, they're gonna give you all kinds of trouble. Can you strongly handle it?" And Jackie said, "Yes," and then Branch Rickey slapped him upside the head. And Jackie's response was, "I've got two cheeks, Mr. Rickey." So that was always a conversation that stood out for me and helped me get back on track. It's so powerful. I wanted to be like those two guys because they knew exactly where they were going. I knew where I was going too, and I knew that a big part of what I was doing was making it easier for people to follow along after I had walked through a given door so that they could walk through it, too. That's always been where I've been going in my life. So what I would say to younger people is, make sure you know where you're going. Yes, static used to bother me, but that was a long time ago. I tell young people, "Don't let it bother you. You know, there are going to be blockers, and there are going to be haters. Don't let it keep you from doing what you want to do. Keep your eye on where you want to go and what you want to give."

Those powerful words from Jim reminded me that this eleventh commandment—making diversity, equity, and inclusion both a personal and organizational advantage—intersects powerfully with the tenth commandment I shared with you, about giving. Jim is all about giving. His personal example highlights the reality that any mission worth pursuing is, ultimately, about service to others. As Jim put it during our interview:

I went to some good schools—I was fortunate in that regard—and this whole idea of finding ways to give back really, for me, started there. That's where I started to see the power of relationships in action. I saw how people worked together and invested time and energy and attention in certain kids and looked for opportunities to help them. And when I saw that, I said to myself, "Damn. This really is part of the secret of success." So very early on, that became a priority for me, and frankly, it was already part of my personality, because I like people. I mean, if you genuinely like people, this is not a huge leap to make. You start looking for ways to help them. You start looking for ways to form relationships, and you start looking for ways to maintain and support those relationships over time. So that's what I do. And you know what? I collect IOUs along the way. There is nothing in the world wrong with that. That's part of how this works. That's part of the mission.

I'll give you an example of what I'm talking about. The other day I get a call from a very powerful guy at a very powerful company, a good friend of mine. He says to me, "Jim, there's this young guy, and I've known his family for a long time. We vacation with them in Jamaica every year. He's interested in going into consulting. Would you talk to him?" Now, technically, do I have time to talk to that friend of a friend? Some people might think the answer is no. I might think the answer is no. But am I going to turn my friend down? Absolutely not. So, I'm helping people and I'm supporting the relationships, just as a matter of course, every chance I get. That's not in question. I'm also collecting an IOU. And you know what? Over the years, I've collected more IOUs than I could ever possibly use. So how do you think I spend those? For decades, I've invested those IOUs in helping people of color get their chance to climb the ladder. From my very early time at McKinsey, that's what I was trying to do. I wanted more people who looked like me to show up in meetings. I looked for ways to make that happen. And a lot of times, I found a way.

What I love about Jim is the way he adds *value* to every relationship and at the same time never loses sight of the *values* that drive his personal mission: creating wealth for minorities.

"As we lose ourselves in the service of others, we discover our own lives and our own happiness."

—Dieter F. Uchtdorf

What is *your* personal mission? You need to know, because that's what you have to be motivated to return to every single time you run into static, roadblocks, or difficult decisions. In fact, the decisions aren't as difficult when you know who you are and what your mission is. It serves as your compass, your guiding light. Do you know your mission/purpose? If not, you need to be ready to focus with clarity, and in an instant, on that mission—on the value you add, on the values you uphold, on the people you intend to serve, and on the relationships you intend to support over time. When wise people talk about changing the world by changing yourself first, they are talking about *you getting clear about your personal mission!* That is the best, and I believe the only, way to turn diversity, equity, and inclusion from a string of buzzwords into a practical daily reality—a way of living.

43. A VOICE TO BE HEARD

"If you haven't hired a team of people who are of color, female, and/or LGBT to actively turn over every stone, to scope out every nook and cranny, to pop out of every bush, to find every qualified underrepresented founder in this country, you're going to miss out on a lot of money when the rest of the investment world gets it."

—*Arlan Hamilton*

A couple of my close friends told me how powerful an experience it was for them to read Jim Lowry's story about Jackie Robinson and Branch Rickey. That story has always meant a lot to me, too, and not just because it shines a light on the personal and spiritual commitment those men had to their personal values. Another reason that story resonates strongly for me is that *baseball* has always been a big part of my life.

I've told you a lot about my mom, including how she used to enlist my help in roasting peanuts to sell at big league ballparks. Indeed, baseball games were a major part of her business plan. She recruited neighborhood teens to help her sell roasted peanuts at Cleveland Indians games. She paid these teens (fairly, I want to emphasize!) to work the stands on game days. My brother and I were jealous of her and the others for being able to go out and see the ball games. We kept lobbying for her to take us to a game. After a whole lot of pleading, my mom finally agreed, on the condition that we work just like she and the other guys making their rounds in the stands were working. We agreed—but once game day rolled around, when we got past the initial joy of being inside a big league ballpark, my brother and I realized that we'd signed up for a *whole lot* of work! We were happy we'd come with her, though, and happy to be part of the experience. After that first day, we both wanted to go back, and because we'd worked hard, my mom let us. The point is, baseball was part of how we as a family earned extra income. It was not just entertainment. So it seems to make sense to share a few more true baseball stories that connect with diversity, equity, and inclusion here. The first true story is about someone you may already have heard of: the Hall of Fame outfielder Lou Brock.

In 1964, Lou Brock, one of the top prospects in the major leagues, was traded from the Chicago Cubs to the St. Louis Cardinals. Why? According to some accounts, it was at least in part because the senior leadership in the Cubs organization felt they had, by that point, signed more than enough Black players. They had "checked the box." They had done what they were supposed to do. And some season ticket holders were complaining that there were too many Black players on the field.

So the day came when the Cubs sent Brock, who had been scouted and brought up through their minor league system by the legendary Buck O'Neil, to St. Louis. The deal is now regarded as one of the worst trades in big league history.

Brock hit .251 for the Cubs that year. He hit .348 for the Cardinals. He would later say of his time in Chicago: "It was like being in a prison yard with everyone waiting for you to do something wrong. There was the thrill, yes, of coming to the major leagues—but I was scared to death."

In St. Louis, the environment was different. Brock was given a starting job and the opportunity and resources he needed to live up to his potential. He made the most of that opportunity and those resources. And not coincidentally, the Cardinals won the World Series twice during his tenure with them.

> "Inclusivity means not just 'we're allowed to be there,' but 'we are valued.' I've always said: smart teams will do amazing things, but truly diverse teams will do impossible things."
>
> —Claudia Brind-Woody

Now: Why do I tell you this story?

Because the organizations we lead—the *lives* we lead—inevitably face a choice: we can operate like the '64 Cubs, who were imprisoned by their own dysfunctional choices in a status quo that was clearly broken, or we can operate like the '64 Cardinals, who were building a brand-new "way we do things here."[18]

One more thing: You will run into some people who tell you that the Cubs failed to make the World Series for well over half a century because of some nonsense involving a fan with a goat being asked to leave Wrigley Field in 1945. That's mythmaking. That's deflection. That's denial. The reality is that the Cubs lagged behind the rest of the National League for one reason and one reason alone: at a critical point in history when they had the chance to take full advantage of the talent that was available to them, they chose not to. And they chose to condone, rather than challenge, a racially hostile working environment. Choosing to create myths about outcomes that are actually under our control is not courage; in fact, it is cowardice. If leaders choose not to take full advantage of the talent that is available to them, that choice is on the leadership and no one else. We should not make up myths to justify the substantial competitive disadvantage that inevitably results. We should change the way we recruit, onboard, train, and retain so that we hire and develop the best people. No urban legend we come up with will change that reality.

> If leaders choose not to take full advantage of the talent that is available to them, that is on the leadership and no one else.

Toxic choices, like the Cubs' decision to maintain a bankrupt and outdated status quo, can have negative impacts for decades. Ask yourself: Is that toxic dynamic limited to Major League Baseball organizations in the 1960s? Or do today's executives have something important to learn from this story?

Discrimination and prejudice are obstacles, not just to personal growth, but to *organizational* growth and success. And whether the organization in question is a company, or a nonprofit organization, or a branch of the government, or a non-governmental organization, *discrimination and prejudice will hold it back*. And diversity, equity, and inclusion will move the organization forward. That's the truth. And those who ignore it or try to pretend it does not apply to them will be left behind in the 21st-century economy.

Here's one more true, powerful baseball story I want to share. It's a story about a young woman on the move and on the rise. Her name is Kiona Sinks, and she currently serves as community engagement manager and director of digital marketing strategy for the Negro

Leagues Baseball Museum in Kansas City, Missouri, an institution founded over three decades ago by Negro Leagues and Major League legend Buck O'Neil, who was recently elected posthumously to the National Baseball Hall of Fame.

> "The most important thing is to learn to bet on yourself so you can make something that lasts."
>
> —Kiona Sinks

Kiona is a relentless social and civic innovator who is busily setting a new standard for how young leaders can model inclusive community engagement through passionate action. The "Black Excellence Kansas City" nonprofit she founded received honors from the Women Future Conference as the Multicultural Campaign of the Year in 2019. In 2020, she signed on with the Museum, where she oversees and manages community and educational partnerships while setting and executing the Museum's cutting-edge social media and digital marketing strategies. Her academic background is nearly as impressive as her professional accomplishments: Kiona helped spearhead the founding of the inaugural African American Student Union (AASU) at Central Methodist University, located in Fayette, Missouri. In just a very short time in Kansas City, Kiona has advanced the agenda for many diverse and marginalized groups and has made a major impact by helping to educate the next generation of leaders on the importance of diversity and inclusion, civic engagement, and social justice. I was struck by her ability to instantly change one's perspectives on what community activism can look like in the modern world and what it can model for people of all backgrounds and perspectives. Kiona is definitely a voice to be heard. Some highlights of our discussion follow.

What got you interested in diversity, equity, and inclusion?

For me, it was a question of moving past whatever struggles had presented themselves and finding a way to do something important, something with a legacy, something that would last and that would be of benefit for the generations to come. I believe troubles don't last. Legacy is what lasts. My grandmother raised me until I was 12; I slept on the couch a lot, and yes, we had some hardships, but I always knew who I was, I knew I was loved, and I knew that the most important thing is to learn to bet on yourself so you can make something that lasts. And I believe that goes for both the individual and the community. The worst people can tell you is "no." You just keep moving forward, as an individual and as a community. Having the courage to move ahead, past whatever obstacles happen to be in front of you—that's what matters. I was always drawn to the possibility of creating that kind of forward motion; that's what cultivated my passion for driving social and civic innovation in ways that maybe hadn't been tried before. And it is such an honor for me that that passion has led me to work for a place with a truly powerful mission like the Negro Leagues Baseball Museum.

What is that mission?

We are the world's only museum dedicated to preserving and celebrating the rich history of African American baseball and its impact on the social advancement of America. I think, unfortunately, it took the catalyst of the passing of George Floyd for a national audience to begin to really understand the importance of what we are doing here in Kansas City. We are a civil rights museum, and we tell our stories through the lens of baseball. This is an intergenerational conversation about people who moved society forward for us—a conversation that we don't have often enough. And since I've come on board, I've been able to see how the museum digitally can take the historical essence of our message, and still be true to what that message means, but also put it out to a newer generation that is now ready and eager to learn about the historic and cultural impact of the Negro Leagues as a catalyst for social change in the United States. And for young people, like me, I see that they are really starting to embrace that history as an important part of their heritage. Their reactions are very strong and very personal. They say things like "How did I not know this?" The stories we tell here are really resonating with young people. Young people are honoring their own heritage by listening to the stories, sharing the stories, and applying them to the future that they intend to build. It's very inspiring, because what we are doing online now through digital platforms actually draws on and continues a very old tradition of storytelling in our community. That's a powerful form of activism, storytelling.

It certainly is. Who's your hero when it comes to the storytelling variety of activism?

I have a lot of heroes, but one who definitely stands out is Bob Kendrick, the president of the Museum. I'm fortunate to have the opportunity to work with and be recognized by someone who just believes in me unconditionally, whether I work for the Museum or not. And Bob is definitely a master storyteller, which anyone who follows his podcast *Black Diamonds* knows.

How did you two meet?

He gave a tour of the Museum to the founding charter members of the African American Student Union at Central Methodist University. That's how we connected. Since then we have always kept in contact. They day I met him, he said, "If you ever make Kansas City home, you know, always feel free to stop by to say, 'Hello.'" Well, I did. I volunteered for five years for the Museum. And our slogan is, "If you stay around long enough, you'll get put to work." So I got put to work. Bob has been much more than a mentor to me. He's been a sponsor. He's made such immense investments in my growth as a person and as a professional that honestly, I don't think I can ever repay the debt. He always tells me, "I want the best for you, no matter where you work. That's never going to change." That's inspiring on a couple of levels: one, it makes me feel a deep commitment to the mission he's taken on; and two, it gives me a role model. I want to make that kind of difference in someone's life too. I want to find a way to pay it forward. That's an important part of activism as well, I think.

YOU ARE A VOICE TO BE HEARD, NOT A BOX TO BE CHECKED.

I have been telling audiences for years: "I am a voice to be heard, not a box to be checked." So are you. We all are. We each have a purpose to understand, a mission to undertake, and values to guide us as we move forward. We are each born to speak and act courageously about our purpose, our mission, and our values, and we deserve to be heard when we do. That right to be heard is, in my view, non-negotiable. And our organizations inevitably gain in strength, impact, potential, and performance to the degree that they acknowledge that right.

So: Let us realize our full potential. Let us act with the knowledge that human potential is the ultimate asset. Let us make sure we are voices to be heard, not boxes to be checked. And let us fix the status quo whenever we see that it is broken. Let us initiate, appropriately, the difficult conversations when we clearly see that it is time to do so. Let us use our voices and our actions to make diversity, equity, and inclusion a personal and competitive advantage for ourselves, our organizations, and our society. And let us use the power of our own purpose, our own mission, and our own values to move the discussion of what is possible forward. That, in my experience, is the direction the best discussions always go. Forward. Always forward. Courageously.

Courageously pursuing a mission that is driven by your personal calling, a mission that is in keeping with your values, is what delivers joy, fulfillment, and purpose. Remember: Fortune always favors the brave.

"Develop enough courage so that you can stand up for yourself and then stand up for somebody else."

—Maya Angelou

44. BEFORE YOU MOVE ON TO THE EPILOGUE, DO THIS

QUESTIONS: COMMANDMENT XI

- Think back to your calling—your big WHY. Whom does your calling serve? How does your calling serve them? What specific outcomes and experiences are you trying to create for the people your calling serves?

- What are the "rules of the road" you are personally committed to following in serving those people? What are you willing to promise that you will always do? What are you willing to promise that you will never do?

- Are you still taking personal private time—time just to be quiet, all by yourself—each day? If not, please re-engage with this commitment to build up the Courage to Hear, the Courage to Dream Big, and the Courage to Do the Right Thing. Today, make a point of using this time to be quiet and mindful about *what your calling looks like in action*. In addition, be quiet and mindful about the "rules of the road" you will definitely follow as you pursue that calling.

ACTIONS: COMMANDMENT XI

- Use the answers you developed to the questions above to create a one-sentence expression of what your personal calling looks like in action. This is your mission statement. Be sure it identifies some form of service to other people.

- Use the answers you developed to the questions above to create a list of between three and seven "rules of the road" that you are willing to commit to unconditionally. These are your personal values. Be sure to include a sentence or two for each value you identify that explains exactly what you mean by it—how you define it, what you associate with it, and/or what it looks like in action.

- Remember: Courageously pursuing a mission that is driven by your personal calling—a mission that is in keeping with your values—is what delivers joy, fulfillment, and purpose.

- Remember: Fortune favors the brave.

Once you have done all this, you will be ready to move on to the Epilogue.

Epilogue

INTEGRITY

We hear a lot of talk these days about integrity. To close this book, I want to ask you to consider an important question: What does that word *integrity* really mean?

The dictionary tells us that *integrity* is "the state of being complete or whole."[19] I believe personal integrity is a matter of being complete and whole as a person...by showing courage in these three dimensions:

Courage in listening without judgment to yourself, meaning the voice within, and to others. Recall how often I have emphasized taking quiet time to yourself and cultivating the courage to hear your own inner voice. Once you learn to listen to yourself without judgment, and not before, you can begin to listen to others without judgment. Accepting what others have to offer without constructing a narrative of victimhood, rescue, or persecution around what we hear is not always easy. In fact, it is the work of a lifetime for most of us. I believe that fact makes it more important for us to strive to master this dimension of courage, not less. Our courage in listening is what defines us in the moment.

Courage in dreaming big and taking action on those dreams. There is something amazing that you and you alone were born to do. There is something ahead of you that only you can define, something that demands the very best from you, something that challenges you to set aside your fears so you can learn, grow, and contribute at levels you might have once considered impossible. All eleven of the commandments I have shared with you in this book have pointed you, in one way or another, toward the goal of identifying and pursuing that personal quest of yours. Remember: The dreaming and the pursuing are what matter most—not the outcome. T. S. Eliot may have captured the essence of this dimension of courage when he wrote, "For us, there is only the trying. The rest is not our business."[20] Our courage in dreaming and acting is what inspires us.

Courage in doing what you know is right. Whenever you take a stand for something because you know, deep down inside, that *not* taking a stand would be a violation of who you are and who you are meant to be, you are living courageously in this dimension. Of course, it is easy to do the right thing when doing the right thing is popular. Doing the right thing when there are consequences and opposition is what makes for a life of true contribution, a life that extends its impact beyond our own, a life that moves everyone forward. Your courage in doing the right thing, in speaking up at the right moment, in not being silent when your voice needs to be heard, is what determines your legacy. Your voice is like a drop of water: each moment you use it to do what you know is right, that half-full glass of water gets a little fuller.

(By the way: If you happen to be a leader within your organization, I hope you will take a close look at the Special Appendix for Courageous Leaders that appears at the end of this book.)

Now it is nearly time to close this book. Ever since I started this project, I promised myself I would close out *Courage By Design* by telling you this: Every once in a while, I think about the fact that my mother, Helen, is no longer with us, and a deep sadness comes over me. I wish she were here to see everything I am up to.

Not long ago, I was one of a group of women investors who rang the opening bell of the New York Stock Exchange. We made the news. It was a bittersweet experience for me, though, because my mom never got to see me do that, and I know she would have loved to have seen it. When I think about the fact that Helen didn't live to share that day with me, a deep sense of loss comes over me.

I mention all this because *every time I feel that sadness, that sense of loss, I try to find a way to put it to use.* So I need you to know, before we say goodbye, that I know I am standing on the shoulders of a giant. This woman was the rock of my life. This was someone who knew fear and pain, yet loved, lived, and made a difference anyway. I will never know all the trials she endured, all the suffering she accepted, all the struggles she overcame to make my journey possible. I think we all have someone like that in our lives. And when we lose them, there are no words to express the pain of that loss.

I have learned that whenever we feel that kind of loss, it can actually empower us—as long as we are using that person's example to empower others. That is what I have tried to do in these pages.

Now Helen is my angel. Now she can help me in ways that she couldn't on this earth.

I suspect there is someone like Helen in your life, someone to whom you owe a debt you can never possibly repay. My final challenge to you is to honor that person by designing and living a courageous life... the kind of life that empowers someone else in the way that person empowered you.

When you do that, your angel will hear a bell ring. Just like I know mine did.

I pray that this book serves as a roadmap to all three of the pathways to integrity I have shared with you. I pray that it helps you to design and live a life of bold, tenacious contribution. I pray that it inspires you to remember the people who made your courageous journey possible, to honor their love for you, and to pay that love forward on their behalf.

Please keep in touch. Email me at dee@couragebydesign.com to share your courageous journey.

Notes

1. Rep. John Lewis quoted in Joshua Bote, "'Get in Good Trouble, Necessary Trouble': Rep. John Lewis in His Own Words," *USA Today*, last updated July 19, 2020, https://www.usatoday.com/story/news/politics/2020/07/18/rep-john-lewis-most-memorable-quotes-get-good-trouble/5464148002/.

2. Rachel Perry, "5 Surprising Facts about Hunger in America," *United Way Blog*, October 15, 2019, https://www.unitedway.org/blog/5-surprising-facts-about-hunger-in-america.

3. "First Say to Yourself What You Would Be," BrainyQuote, n.d., https://www.brainyquote.com/quotes/epictetus_161531.

4. "Seek Not the Good in External Things," AZ Quotes, n.d., https://www.azquotes.com/quote/390130.

5. "There Is Only One Way to Happiness," BrainyQuote, n.d., https://www.brainyquote.com/quotes/epictetus_121546.

6. "Any Person Capable of Angering You Becomes Your Master," Goodreads, n.d., https://www.goodreads.com/quotes/135630-any-person-capable-of-angering-you-becomes-your-master-he.

7. "It's Not What Happens to You, But How You React to It That Matters," BrainyQuote, n.d., https://www.brainyquote.com/quotes/epictetus_149126.

8. "My Story," ValentinoDixon.com, n.d., https://www.valentinodixon.com/my-story.

9. Kori D. Miller, "The Psychology and Theory Behind Flow," PositivePsychology.com, last updated December 14, 2021, https://positivepsychology.com/theory-psychology-flow/.

10. Arthur O'Shaughnessy, "Ode," Poetry Foundation, https://www .poetryfoundation.org/poems/54933/ode-.

11. Madeleine Albright, "Madeleine Albright: My Undiplomatic Moment," *The New York Times*, February 12, 2016, https://www .nytimes.com/2016/02/13/opinion/madeleine-albright-my -undiplomatic-moment.html.

12. Melanie Curtin, "Winston Churchill's 12-Word Definition of Success May Just Change Your Life," Inc.com, n.d., https://www.inc .com/melanie-curtin/in-just-12-words-winston-churchill-gives-us -a-definition-of-success-that-could-outlast-them-all.

13. Michael Winerip, "Building a Golf Course and Beating Racism," *The New York Times*, June 28, 1996, https://archive.nytimes.com/ www.nytimes.com/specials/canton/0628canton.html.

14. Jade Scipioni, "Colin Powell: 'Get Mad, and Then Get Over It,' and 12 Other Rules He Lived and Worked By," CNBC, last updated October 18, 2021, https://www.cnbc.com/2021/10/18/black -american-trailblazer-colin-powells-13-rules-for-life-and-work .html.

15. "Maximizing Mentoring and Securing Sponsorship," Webinar from Catalyst, September 24, 2015, https://www.catalyst.org/research/ webinar-recording-maximizing-mentoring-and-securing -sponsorship/.

16. *It's a Wonderful Life*, directed by Frank Capra (1947; Hollywood, CA: RKO Radio Pictures, 2004), Streaming.

17. William Ballard, "The Keys to Riches and Wealth," Medium, February 9, 2017, https://wbenterprise.medium.com/the-key-to -riches-and-wealth-b5e88448ca74.

18. See Steve Bogira, "Unfriendly Confines: Did Racial Discrimination Start the Cubs' Slide?" Chicago Reader, March 24, 2014, https:// chicagoreader.com/news-politics/unfriendly-confines-did-racial -discrimination-start-the-cubs-slide/.

19. *Merriam-Webster*, s.v. "integrity," https://www.merriam-webster .com/dictionary/integrity.

20. T. S. Eliot, *Four Quartets*, II.V.18, Philoctetes.org, n.d., http:// philoctetes.org/documents/Eliot%20Poems.pdf.

Special Appendix

FOR COURAGEOUS LEADERS

I f you lead a team or an organization, let me challenge you to use the following questions and action steps to become a more courageous leader—and to build a more courageous organization.

Question: Are you ready, willing, and able to make the case to senior leadership in your organization for a deeper and more comprehensive commitment to diversity, equity, and inclusion? If your answer is *yes*, what steps are you willing to take *today*? If your answer is *no*, why not?

Action: Learn the documented bottom-line competitive advantages of diversity, equity, and inclusion. Share those with your organization's senior leadership.

- An influential study from McKinsey reported that companies with higher than 30 percent female executives were more likely to outperform companies where this percentage ranged from 10 to 30 percent. The study also found that these 10-to-30-percent companies, in turn, were more likely to outperform organizations with even fewer women executives, or with none at all.[1]

---

1 McKinsey & Company, "Diversity Wins: How Inclusion Matters," May 19, 2020, *McKinsey.com*, https://www.mckinsey.com/featured-insights/diversity-and-inclusion/diversity-wins-how-inclusion-matters.

- The McKinsey study also found that companies in the top quartile for ethnic and cultural diversity in the executive team were 36 percent more likely to post above-average profitability results than companies in the bottom quartile.[2]

- Results like these—and there are many, many more studies confirming the bottom-line advantages of DEI—demonstrate powerfully that women and minorities are not a box to be checked but an asset to be leveraged. Make the case to your company's leadership. Point out how strange it is that the "fight" for inclusion should have to be a fight at all, when the data so overwhelmingly reveals DEI's role in enhancing financial performance.

Question: Who else in your organization knows how important DEI is? Make a list of people *outside* the DEI team who are making this a priority. Who else wants to see the organization walk its talk on this issue? Who is willing to take action? Add as many names to your list as you can.

Action: Build a constituency for accountability within your organization on the issue of DEI. Invite people on your list to lunch. Talk about this issue. Make sure there is more than one advocate for internal change. Make sure the advocates are staying in touch with each other on a regular basis. Share your concerns and your action plans. Reach across silos; make a point of engaging in real time with other leaders who know this needs to be a priority.

---

2   Ibid.

Question: Is quantifiable progress toward DEI metrics part of the annual executive compensation review picture? If not, why not? Who within your organization can make sure these metrics are tied directly to financial rewards for your organization's leadership team?

Action: Get executive compensation reform on the agenda. If you run into a brick wall on making DEI part of the executive compensation review picture, ask this question: "Why does the principle of 'you can't measure what you can't manage' seem to apply to everything *except* our organization's DEI initiative?" Metrics you can use include the following: pipelines of promotable people for key leadership roles, benchmark promotion tracking, hiring trends, mentorships, recruitment colleges contacted, and hiring mandates implemented. Only when leaders know that they will be reviewed based on those kinds of metrics will businesses start driving real outcomes.

Question: When you hire women and minority candidates, how do you support them after the hire? What kind of coaching and training do they receive? What mentorship and sponsorship opportunities do they get to take advantage of? Do people in non-leadership positions receive the support they need in the critical 90-day period after a hire? If so, what kind? If not, why not?

Action: Invest in women and minority hires *after* they get the job. Don't stop with the hire. It simply doesn't make any sense at all to spend money to bring qualified people in and then abandon them. Choose to invest in the talent. Get the most out of your hires: give them the resources, mentorship, and sponsorship they need, *no matter what part of the company they work in*, and make sure they are working in an environment that values and supports them.

Question: Do you personally coach women and minority applicants you can't hire right now? Do you ask if you can give them feedback on how they could improve their chances next time? Do you offer constructive criticism? Do you stay in touch over time? Do you forward employment leads and other introductions that may be of interest? If not, why not?

Action: Coach and sponsor women and minority candidates who aren't quite ready yet. Let them know you've got their back. See yourself in them. Odds are, you needed a hand too at some point in your career—and got a hand. Now is your chance to pay it forward! Mentorship is not sponsorship. Sponsorship is what we need.

Question: Who's at the table? When you go out to lunch, do all the people who come along with you to the restaurant look and sound like you? When you convene a meeting to discuss an important issue, does everyone who is asked to be at that meeting look and sound like you? If so, how can you broaden the diversity of thought and experience at these gatherings—and give your team and your organization a competitive advantage? Are the people in charge of your DEI initiative empowered and given the authority, and the budget, to effect meaningful organizational change?

Action: Drive fear out of your organization. Empower people to speak up, take risks, share their personal experience, and add value to the organization. Reward them for doing so. Promote a culture and an environment of inclusion. Lead by example in this area by reaching out to people who don't look and sound like you and encouraging them to join social occasions and important business discussions. Become mindful of your own actions, and be aware of the unintended consequences of discussions that may alienate or silence team members. For instance: You tell one team member that you had a nice chat with his dad, a college buddy of yours. Will that remark make other people on your team feel that they don't have access to the same level of opportunity, or the same ability to be heard, as the person whose father you consider a friend?

Do the right thing. Take personal responsibility to act, and act *now*. The time for half-hearted measures is over. Expand your personal and organizational courage by taking each of these actions *today*. As a leader, you have the power to influence lives. Step up and claim that responsibility. Take these actions *now*, and make sure that each one of your team members, at all levels, feels valued. Our organizations simply can't afford to keep doing the same thing and expecting a different result.

Acknowledgments

I extend my deep gratitude to the following special people for the help, support, guidance, patience, love, and yes, courage they committed to this project.

Thank you to David Wildasin, whom I happened to meet on a fateful air journey three years ago, who pushed me when I needed pushing, and without whom this book would never have seen the light of day; to Jennifer Janechek, who did such a magnificent job on the editing; and to the entire Sound Wisdom team.

I am also grateful to the Hudson News partners and team, whose support for this project has made a huge difference.

Deep thanks go out to my friend Jerry Greenfield; to my C200 sisters Lisa Stone, Monica Cole, Shellye Archambeau, Karen Van Bergen, and Kay Koplovitz; and to Renee Powell, Jim Lowry, Isabelle Freidheim, Valentino Dixon, Kiona Sinks, and Congressman Jim Clyburn, all of whom contributed in important ways to the development of this book.

Vernessa Gates, Tess Snipes, Michelle Rogers, Hedy Ratner, Alisa Starks, Griselda Walls, Connie Merritt, Mitchell Heskel, Jesse Johnson, Carlton Guthrie and Greg White, I thank you all for your friendship and your moral support.

Thanks go out, too, to all the dear friends and family members who have made my life far richer just by being part of it. I can't list you all here, but you know who you are, and I hope you know I appreciate you from the bottom of my heart. To my father Pezavia Wheeler, my twin brother Dr. Skip Robinson, and my daughter Danielle Robinson, thank you for the blessing of you. Finally, I must point out that all that I share in this book ultimately connects to my mother, Helen Hill, and that it is to her that I owe the deepest debt and gratitude.

Meet

DEE M. ROBINSON

Growth strategist, entrepreneurial innovator, DE&I advocate, social impact leader, and venture capitalist **Dee M. Robinson** believes we can all lead with passion and leave people and places better than we found them—and that we all have the power to use courage to influence people and outcomes. She is committed to shattering expectations, redefining the status quo, creating value, making good trouble, and empowering women and people of color.

She is the CEO and president of Robinson Hill, Inc., a food and beverage/retail concessions management firm she founded in 1995. Dee has scaled the company's operations by forging successful joint ventures and partnerships, which now encompass airport restaurants and retail stores across the United States. She is also the founder and CEO of GT Spirits, maker of Good Trouble bourbon; proceeds from the sale of Good Trouble support a variety of social justice causes. Dee has been featured in such publications as *Forbes, Crain's Chicago Business, Chicago Sun-Times, WayMaker Journal, Enterprising Women,* and *Medium.*

Dee serves on several company boards, including Accel Entertainment, Wintrust Bank, and Athena Consumer Acquisition Corp., one of the first entirely women-run SPACs. She is a trustee of PGA REACH and a board member of C200. She has been recognized as a

HistoryMaker, Chicago United Business Leader of Color, WomenInc's Most Influential Corporate Director, and is the recipient of the Fellowship Open's National Civic Award.

JOIN THE COURAGE COMMUNITY!

Find resources to support your courageous journey at
www.couragebydesign.com.

Sign up for the newsletter at
www.couragebydesign.com.

Share your story by emailing
dee@couragebydesign.com.

CONNECT WITH DEE ON SOCIAL MEDIA

#CourageCircle #CourageCommunity #CourageByDesign

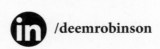 **/deemrobinson**

 **@deemrobinson**

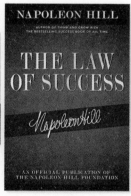